GOD SUFFERS FOR US

A SYSTEMATIC INQUIRY INTO A CONCEPT
OF DIVINE PASSIBILITY

GOD SUFFERS FOR US

A SYSTEMATIC INQUIRY INTO A CONCEPT
OF DIVINE PASSIBILITY

by

JUNG YOUNG LEE

MARTINUS NIJHOFF / THE HAGUE / 1974

231.4
Su 28l

201876

ACKNOWLEDGMENTS

Anyone who is well acquainted with contemporary theological thought will immediately come to recognize my debt to numerous scholars in the past and present. While it is almost impossible to give an adequate acknowledgment to all those who have contributed directly or indirectly in the preparation of this work, I cannot fail to mention my former teacher and friend, Dean J. Robert Nelson, under whose supervision basic researches for this book were carried out several years ago. Without his inspiration and encouragement this study was not possible. I also acknowledge my indebtedness to the faculty and students of Boston University School of Theology, to whom this book is gratefully dedicated. Finally, I would like to express my thanks to the University of North Dakota for the Faculty Research Grant, which assisted me to complete this book.

Jung Young Lee
Grand Forks, North Dakota

Dedicated To
THE FACULTY AND STUDENTS
OF
BOSTON UNIVERSITY SCHOOL OF THEOLOGY
IN THE FELLOWSHIP OF LEARNING

—

FOREWORD

Dietrich Bonhoeffer, writing in his cell in a Nazi prison, expressed a most remarkable idea. "Men go to God in His need." This is the insight, he observed, which distinguishes the Christian faith from all other religions. It is a universal belief that God, or the gods, should come to help man in his mortal, human need. But this is not the God and Father of Jesus Christ. Even as Jesus in Gethsemane chided his disciples for their sloth in not keeping watch with him during his agony, so God the Father must look to His creatures for their faith and sympathy. Therein lies the basis for the Christian answer to mankind's perennial complaint: Why do men suffer?

Not all theologians, believing Christians, or believers in a personal God can share this idea. Traditionally the Eastern Orthodox thinkers have adhered to the rule of apophatic theology: that is, there are boundaries of knowledge about God which the human mind, even when enlightened by revelation, cannot cross. So who can say that God the Eternal One is susceptible to what we call suffering? It is better to hold one's silence on so deep a mystery. Still others are loathe to acknowledge God's passibility for varying reasons. God is ultimate and perfect; therefore he cannot know suffering or other emotions. God is impersonal; therefore it is meaningless to ascribe personal, anthropopathic feelings to Him.

Many angels may fear to tread on the ground of this most difficult question. But Dr. Lee (though hardly a fool!) has rushed in to grapple with the issue. His investigation is an intellectual *tour de force,* bold in purpose and original in conception. Its main value for theological knowledge lies in its unveiling of the several very significant implications of the doctine of God's passibility. While some might object that the whole question is beyond human grasp, he has shown that there is sufficient understanding of it to illuminate other more familiar questions, such as evil, atonement, incarnation, and the Trinity. And if Dr. Lee's theological reach seems to exceed his grasp, that's what heaven's for.

J. Robert Nelson
Dean & Professor of Systematic Theology
Boston University School of Theology

TABLE OF CONTENTS

INTRODUCTION

The concept of divine suffering is not only the core of our faith but the uniqueness of Christianity. Nevertheless, it has been not only denied by the early Church but almost completely ignored in important theological works of our time. Dietrich Bonhoeffer alluded to the significance of this idea but never actualized it in his theology.

In 1924 J. K. Mozley had pointed out how completely the issue of divine passibility was ignored in many theological works where one might have expected at least some mention of the word "impassibility."[1] He was deeply disillusioned that responsible theologians in the nineteenth and early twentieth centuries had kept an extensive silence on the problem of divine pathos, while they had devoted much attention to the question of the divine will and purpose for the world. Almost a half century later, Paul Tillich has expressed a similar concern over the problem of divine passibility. In the last volume of his *Systematic Theology* he states that present-day theology tries to avoid the issue of divine passibility, "either by ignoring it or by calling it an inscrutable divine mystery."[2] "But such escape," he says, "is impossible in view of the question's significance for the most existential problem of theodicy .... If theology refuses to answer such existential questions, it has neglected its task."[3] In spite of these remarks, he proceeds to give it only two pages out of nearly 1,000. Thus Woollcombe rightly reproves that Tillich himself has failed to deal with this problem.[4] It is quite apparent, then, that the study underlying the present book is an attempt to fill the striking need for a fresh re-examination of a concept of divine passibility. Before we take any definite step toward the strategy of this investigation, let us make a brief survey of important writings on the question of divine passibility in the twentieth century.

The concept of divine passibility had been rejected by the early and

---

[1] J. K. Mozley, *The Impassibility of God: A Survey of Christian Thought* (Cambridge: Cambridge University Press, 1926), p. 128.

[2] Paul Tillich, *Systematic Theology,* Vol. III (Chicago: University of Chicago Press, 1973), p. 404.

[3] *Ibid.*

[4] Kenneth Woolcombe, "The Pain of God," *The Scottish Journal of Theology,* Vol. XX, No. 2 (June, 1967), p. 132.

Medieval fathers of the Orthodox Church, including Thomas Aquinas, who believed that God Himself was absolutely impassible. Yet, modern theology, particularly within the Protestant tradition, has significantly returned to the assertion of divine passibility. In 1917, H. Maurice Relton published an article, "Patripassianism,"[5] which gave a comprehensive survey of the patripassian heresy in the early Church and defended it on the basis of Christological significance. One of the most significant contributions in the field was the famous essay of Baron F. von Hügel on "Suffering and God,"[6] which was originally delivered as a lecture to the members of the London Society for the Study of Religion in May, 1921. The traditional doctrine of divine impassibility was well defended by von Hügel on the philosophical ground that God was "Unmixed Joy" and "Entire Delectation." Perhaps one of the most violent oppositions to von Hügel's essay came from Bishop McConnell's "The Wealth of the Divine Feeling" in the twenty-third chapter of his *Is God Limited?*[7] Bishop McConnell's argument was first to repudiate those claims that attributing pain to God would eventually limit Him, and then to assert that God would be limited if pain could not reach Him. In 1926 J. K. Mozley published *The Impassibility of God,*[8] which was an historical survey. Two years later B. R. Brasnett wrote a synthesis in his *The Suffering of the Impassible God*[9] in an attempt to reconcile the sharp division between the concepts of the passibility and impassibility of God. With this book the lively debate during the 1930s was ended without being materialized. For almost ten years after the debate no single significant article appeared which directly dealt with the problem of divine passibility. In 1939, H. Wheeler Robinson published *Suffering, Human and Divine,*[10] which proposes the thesis that the problem of theodicy could only be dealt with satisfactorily through the understanding of the meaning and significance of divine suffering. In 1965 the English translation of Kazoh Kitamori's *Theology of the Pain of God,*[11] which was largely written during World War II, made a unique contribution of Japanese theology to the Western world, even though its use of elliptical logic presented

---

[5] It was first published in *Church Quarterly Review,* July, 1917, and republished as a chapter in Relton's book, *Studies in Christian Doctrine* (London: Macmillan and Company, 1960).

[6] This article is found in von Hügel's *Essays and Addresses on the Philosophy of Religion,* 2nd Series (London: J. M. Dent and Sons, 1926).

[7] Francis J. McConnell, *Is God Limited?* (London: Williams and Norgate, 1924).

[8] This is a survey of Christian thought which was originally written as a doctoral dissertation for the Archbishops' Doctrinal Commission, Cambridge University in 1924 and published in 1926.

[9] Bertrand R. Brasnett, *The Suffering of the Impassible God* (London: S. P. C. K., 1928).

[10] H. Wheeler Robinson, *Suffering, Human and Divine* (New York: Macmillan and Company, 1939).

[11] Kazoh Kitamori, *Theology of the Pain of God.* This is a translation of *Kami no Itami no Shingaku,* published in 1948. The English edition was published in Richmond by John Knox Press, 1965.

some difficulty for a Western mind to follow. He combined the peculiar quality of Japanese tragedy, *tsurasa,* with a Christian concept of the pain of God, which was primarily oriented toward Lutheran theology. Therefore, the strength of Kitamori's theology was in his creative insight of using the original quality of his native expression, while his weakness was in his provincialism in confining himself primarily to Lutheran theology. As Kitamori himself had pointed out, [12] his study was not intended for a systematic treatise but as an exegetical point of view to the content of the biblical message. In recent years a theology of process, following the philosophy of Alfred Whitehead, seems to provide valuable insights to understanding divine passibility. Even though the idea of divine suffering is implicit in the process theology, there is no comprehensive treatise on this topic.

As a result of the brief survey, we are reassured that there is a pressing demand for a comprehensive systematic treatise on the question of divine passibility in our time. In order to fill this striking need of present theology, this study proposes to undertake a systematic inquiry into a concept of divine passibility in the light of contemporary theological insights. Thus the aim of our study is differentiated from either a critical analysis or an historical survey of significant contributions in the field. Our task aims at the constructive and creative approach to apprehend a concept of divine passibility in a systematic fashion.

This study is based on the conviction that God as the Ultimate reality is essentially love, which is "the drive toward the reunion of the separated."[13] This drive for reunion makes God participate in the world. This act of the divine love to participate in the world of sin or the empathy of God creates the possibility of God. Therefore, our first task is to define the nature of God as love, and establish a criterion, the empathy of God, for the divine passibility as a mode of the divine love. Secondly, in order to test the validity of a traditional doctrine of divine impassibility, the basic assumption for this doctrine and some of the serious objections against the assertion of divine passibility are examined in terms of this criterion. Thirdly, through the use of this criterion, we intend to see whether a concept of divine passibility is compatible with the major doctrines of the Christian faith, namely the doctrines of Creation, Incarnation, Atonement, the Holy Spirit and the Trinity. Finally, the practical significance of a concept of divine passibility to a human existential situation is to be investigated. To sum up, we propose in this study (1) to define and apply the empathy of God as the criterion for the assertion of divine passibility, (2) to test the validity of a doctrine of divine impassibility

---

[12] Kazoh Kitamori, *Theology of the Pain of God* (Richmond: John Knox Press, 1965), p. 13.
[13] Paul Tillich, *Systematic Theology,* Vol. III (Chicago: University of Chicago Press, 1963), p. 134.

in terms of this criterion, (3) to examine the compatibility of a concept of divine passibility with major doctrines of the Christian faith, and (4) to apply a concept of divine passibility to the problem of human suffering.

In order to express the pathos of God, which is the basis of divine passibility, meaningfully in terms of human experience, we have chosen the analogy of faith (or the analogy of relation) as the theological method of interpretation. If the God, who makes Himself known to us, is both transcendent and immanent at the same time, what we say about Him cannot be either an equivocity (the same term, applied to two different objects, designates different things in the one and the other), which eliminates the divine immanence, or a univocity (the same term, applied to two different objects, designates the same meaning in both of them), which eliminates the divine transcendence. Out of this tension between the equivocity and univocity, the choice of the analogy, which means a partial correspondence and agreement, is almost inevitable. However, the analogous knowledge of the divine pathos cannot be accessible to us directly from our cognition, for it represents the highest point of contrast with our speculative idea of God.[14] It is knowable to us only indirectly through our faith in God, who is most perfectly manifested in Christ. This is why Paul calls this analogy the analogy of faith (ἀναλογία τῆς πίστεως), which is translated in the Revised Standard Version as "proportion to our faith" (Romans 12:6), since the analogous knowledge of the divine is proportioned to our faith in Christ. The effectiveness of this approach is well demonstrated in the theology of Karl Barth, who combines the cognitive significance of faith in Christ with the dynamic and personal relationship, which exists first in Godhead as the prototype of the "I-Thou" encounter and comes to us as its reflection. The congeniality of this analogy to accomodate a concept of divine passibility is due to its indirect, dynamic, personal and Christological approaches. An extended treatise on the biblical origin, Barth's use and the compatibility of the analogy of faith is devoted in the Appendix of this book. My comprehensive treatise on Barth's use of analogy in his theology has appeared in *The Scottish Journal of Theology*. I am grateful for the permission to use the material in this book.[15]

Finally, a few words concerning the use of terms may prevent any misunderstanding later. The terms "passibility" and "impassibility" are used to designate the capacity or incapacity of God to experience suffering. The word "suffering" is used discriminately from the word "pain," even though they are inseparable in reality. Pain is defined in terms of a sensation bound

---

[14] Emil Brunner, *The Christian Doctrine of God: Dogmatics,* Vol. I, trans. by Olive Wyon (Philadelphia: The Westminster Press, 1950), p. 274.
[15] See Jung Young Lee, "Karl Barth's Use of Analogy in his Church Dogmatics," in *The Scottish Journal of Theology,* Vol. XXII, No. 2 (June, 1969), pp. 129–151.

to the body, while suffering is in terms of a loving relationship bound to time. Thus it is irrelevant to attribute pain to God, who is Spirit. Nevertheless, suffering can be attributed to Him, who loves us in Christ. Suffering can be divided into two categories: voluntary and involuntary suffering. The former is often called redemptive suffering, while the latter is penal suffering. When we attribute suffering to the divine, we mean the former, namely the pure form of vicarious and redemptive suffering. An extended explanation of these terms will be rendered in Chapter I.

A CRITERION FOR THE ASCRIPTION OF DIVINE

PASSIBILITY: THE EMPATHY OF GOD

As we have already stated, our study is based on the conviction that God is love, which is fundamental to the divine pathos. Thus, His love for the world implies that He is passionately involved in the world. The participation of this divine pathos in our life, the empathy of God, becomes a criterion for our understanding of divine passibility. This participation of divine pathos in our life is the very expression of divine nature. If divine nature is *Agape,* the empathy of God is a way of *Agape.* Thus *Agape* becomes the basis of a criterion, a guiding norm of our theological interpretation, for the ascription of passibility to the divine.

The Foundation of a Criterion: Agape *as the Content of the Christian Faith*

In the thirteenth chapter of I Corinthians, Paul beautifully illustrates *Agape* as the essence of the Christian faith. However strong the faith might be, without love it is nothing (I Corinthians 13 : 2). "Faith is indeed simply the vessel which receives the divine love."[1] Faith is analogous to our hand by which we receive love. *Agape,* which is the content of faith, is in reality nothing else than the God who reveals Himself in Christ, for "God is love" (I John 4 : 7). "The content of faith cannot be separated from faith itself."[2] Thus, faith always works through *Agape* (Galatians 5 : 6). *Agape* cannot exist in us without faith or faith without *Agape.* Both *Agape* and faith mutually complement each other. Thus, "Faith is not a vessel which can be filled with any content one likes; it comes into being always simultaneously with its 'content,' with this self-manifestation of God."[3] They are mutually supportive of each other in terms of the form and content, but faith is in some sense dependent entirely

---

[1] Brunner, *Dogmatics, I,* 199.
[2] Gustaf Aulen, *The Faith of the Christian Church,* trans. by E. H. Wahlstrom and G. E. Arden (Philadelphia: The Muhlenberg Press, 1948), p. 92.
[3] Emil Brunner, *The Christian Doctrine of the Church, Faith, and the Consummation: Dogmatics,* Vol. III, trans. by David Cairns in collaboration with T. H. L. Parker (Philadelphia: The Westminster Press, 1960), p. 17.

on *Agape,* since *Agape* is also the subject of faith. Faith is dependent on *Agape,* because it is the temporal form of eternal presence in Christ. On the other hand, *Agape* is the eternal presence of God Himself. It is in this respect not the faith that never fails—"for it disappears with the earthly conditions of life—but love, for it is God Himself."[4] *Agape is not about faith, but faith is about Agape.* "Faith is nothing in itself but the openness of our heart for God's love."[5] In other words, faith is only faith insofar as it is being held by *Agape.* The Christian faith is, then, entirely dependent upon *Agape,* while *Agape* is fulfilled in our faith. Therefore, in the last analysis, the idea of God as *Agape* occupies the center of all the affirmations of Christian faith.

It is quite important to our study to make a clear distinction between the nature and attribute of God. The failure of maintaining this distinction may result in a serious confusion, because the divine nature governs the quality of divine attribute and not vice versa. Thus, if *Agape* is the divine nature and passibility is a divine attribute, the latter must conform to the former. As we have already demonstrated, *Agape* is not only the content of the Christian faith but the center of our affirmation about God. Let us examine further the concept of God's love as the very nature of God who reveals Himself in Christ.

As Brunner has pointed out, it is precisely the failure of the traditional works of dogmatics that they treat the love of God as a divine attribute under the heading of the "ethical attributes."[6] Brunner believes that this kind of arrangement shows the influence of Greek philosophy, which is quite contrary to the biblical idea of *Agape.* The Bible states that *Agape* is not merely God's "temper" or disposition, but it is God's Nature. In other words, *Agape* is not "quality" or the quality of being loving, but it is the very nature of the divine. The Johannine statement, "God is love" (I John 4 : 8, 11), signifies that *Agape* is more than a mere attribute but the very nature of God. Therefore, "the statements, 'God is' and 'God loves' are synonymous. They explain and *confirm one another.'"[7] God loves us, not merely because of His capacity for loving, but because His very being is love. To illustrate it with a Johannine phrase, "He who abides in love, abides in God, and God abides in him" (I John 4 : 16). Thus, God's loving is possible, because He is love in His very existence. It is His very nature to love. In this respect, *Agape* is more than a function of God. Bonhoeffer illustrates it well when he says, "Love is not what He *does* and what He *suffers,* but it is what *He* does and what *He* suffers. Love

[4] Brunner, *Dogmatics, I,* 199.
[5] Emil Brunner, *Faith, Hope, and Love* (Philadelphia: The Westminster Press, 1956), p. 75.
[6] Brunner, *Dogmatics, I,* 191.
[7] Karl Barth, *The Doctrine of Reconciliation (Church Dogmatics),* Vol. IV/2, trans. by G. W. Bromiley (Edinburgh: T. and T. Clark, 1958) ~ 755.

is always He Himself. Love is always God Himself."[8] Bonhoeffer's intention is clearly to show the importance of the *Agape* as the nature of God. Since what God is determines what He does, the *Agape* is inclusive of both God's being and action. If the nature of God is love, His will is none other than the commitment of love and His reason is none other than the structural form of love. In reality love is the ground of divine activity, because it is His own nature of "being."

Agape is mostly known to us as what God does to us rather than what God is in Himself. Thus Ferré, for instance, defines *Agape* as "outgoing concern for fellowship."[9] This overflowing and outgoing concern for others is one of the distinctive functions of *Agape*. As we shall see in the next section of this chapter, the concept of divine empathy as a way of *Agape* is consistent with the idea of outgoing concern as a functional definition of *Agape*. Another distinctive function of *Agape* is to create lovable values in others. This idea is well explained by von Hügel, who says: "A love which loves, not in acknowledgement of an already present lovableness, but in order to render lovable in the future what at present repels love."[10] While *Eros* is directed to the lovable and motivated by the quality of the beloved, *Agape* loves *in spite of* the lovableness or the value of the beloved. *Agape* does not seek value but creates it. In other words, *Agape* creates the lovable in the unlovable.[11] The concept of *Agape* as what God does to us is beautifully summarized by John Baillie.

At the center of everything in Christian religion stands the fact of God's redeeming love; a love that returns not evil on evil but casts over evil the cloak of its forgiveness; a love poured, not on the righteous and self-reliant, but on weak and helpless sinners; a love given, not as a reward of goodness, but in order to creat a goodness which is its own reward; a love that goes out to seek us when we are 'yet a great way off'; a love that stoops to conquer, and humbles itself that we may be exalted; a love that goes with us through the valley of the shadow of death in order that we with it may come forth at last into its own larger life.[12]

We have said so far what the love of God does to us. Let us now focus our attention on what *Agape* is in itself. *Agape* is what God is in Himself; it is more than immanent since God is both immanent and transcendent at the

---

[8]   Dietrich Bonhoeffer, *Ethics* (New York: The Macmillan Company, 1955), p. 174.

[9]   Nels F. S. Ferré, *Evil and the Christian Faith* (New York: Harper and Brothers, 1947), p. 79.

[10]   Baron F. von Hügel, "Morals and Religion," *Essays and Addresses on the Philosophy of Religion,* Second Series (London: J. M. Dent and Sons, 1926), p. 160.

[11]   Anders Nygren, *Agape and Eros,* trans. by Philip S. Watson (Philadelphia: The Westminster Press, 1953), p. 76.

[12]   John Baillie, *The Place of Jesus Christ in Modern Christianity* (New York: Charles Scribner's Sons, 1929), p. 181.

same time. God cannot be conceived in terms of either immanence only or transcendence only but both immanence and transcendence at the same time. Since *Agape* is the nature of God, it must be understood in terms of this dialectical unity between the two opposite poles of divine character. Thus, our understanding of *Agape* includes the holiness of God. This is why we cannot separate the holiness from the love of God.

It is a mistake to separate the holiness from the love of God by saying that God as love is central to the message of the New Testament, while God as holiness is characteristic to that of the Old Testament. As the New Testament is inseparable from the Old Testament, the holiness and love of God are mutually dependent on each other. They are mutually inclusive, because holiness is the holiness of God who is love. The love of God is always the love of the holy God, and the holy God is always love. Love is not love of God if it is not holy. At the same time, holiness is not really holy if it is not love. Holiness is the presupposition of love, while love is the fulfillment of holiness. Therefore, even though there is a sharp contrast between holiness, which creates distance, and love, which creates communion, they are in unity. In other words, in the nature of *Agape* there is a dialectical unity[13] between the transcendental character of love, that is, the holiness of God, and the immanent character of love, that is, God's coming to man. God is both totally immamant and totally transcedent at the same time. A rigid distinction between the holiness and love of God or the transcendence and immanence of God destroys the inner unity of divine disposition. The Johannine concept of God as *Agape* is simultaneously transcendent and immanent. If we really believe that *Agape* is the love of the holy God, it certainly has the element of holiness in itself. Therefore, we conclude that within *Agape* itself there is the transcendent character (or the holiness) of God, which is expressed in the immanent character of God as revealed in Jesus Christ. To illustrate this paradox with Bonhoeffer's words, "The transcendent is not infinitely remote, but close at hand."[14] The real mystery of God as *Agape* is, then, this dialectical unity which can produce the inner tension because of man's sin. This dialectical unity in *Agape* becomes the background for understanding a concept of divine passibility in terms of divine empathy, which is the guiding norm of our theological interpretation.

[13] The paradox of the ultimate reality in terms of dialectical unity between the opposite characters (between transcendence and immanence or between love and holiness) is clearly expressed in the symbols of *Yin* and *Yang* in the diagram of the Great Ultimate or *T'ai Chi T'u* (　太極圖　). See for details in Jung Young Lee, *The Principle of Changes: Understanding the I Ching* (New Hyde Park: University Books, 1971), p. 53 ff.

[14] Dietrich Bonhoeffer, *Prisoner for God: Letters and Papers from Prison* (New York: The Macmillan Company, 1954), p. 175.

A Definition of the Criterion: The Empathy
of God as a Function of Agape

We have attempted to present a sound argument that *Agape,* which is the very nature of God Himself, is not only what God does to us in the world but what God is to Himself. Some of the main characteristics of the manifested form of *Agape,* such as God's self-sacrificial love or His love for His children in spite of their rebellion, seem to imply the actual experience of divine suffering. On the other hand, the dialectical union of both the transcendence and immanence of God in the very nature of *Agape* suggests that there is the possibility of tension, that is, the potentiality of divine passibility, in the inner life of God. Our task here is to define the criterion by which this potentiality may become the actual experience of divine suffering. The actualization of this potentiality implies the transmutation of what *Agape* is in itself to what *Agape* is for the world. Thus, the actual transition takes place with the creation of the world and the fall of man. Because God loves the world, He participated in the world. This participation of love is the empathy of God.

Before defining the empathy of God, let us examine whether the sympathy of God, which is commonly accepted as a criterion for the ascription of divine passibility, is valid. In order to do this, it is necessary to understand the concept of divine sympathy with great clarity.

It has been commonly accepted by most of those who admit the concept of divine passibility that, if God ever suffers, He must suffer in pure sympathy. God, whose nature is perfect and self-sufficient, does not suffer for Himself but suffers vicariously and sympathetically for the suffering of His children. If God is love, He cannot be in His own nature indifferent to the afflictions of His own children. "He consequently identifies Himself with the suffering of His children as they grow."[15] This identification of God with His children is to be understood as the sympathy of God. The legitimate meaning of sympathy is certainly an emotional identification. Sympathy is one's identification of himself with the feeling of others without an actual participation in it. Thus, we question whether the concept of sympathy is compatible with that of *Agape.*

Max Scheler has pointed out that the characteristic feature of sympathy, in comparison to the concept of *Agape,* is always reactive, while love is spontaneous and free from this limitation.[16] In this respect, the sympathy of God, that is, God's identification of His pathos with the suffering of the children,

---

[15] Ferré, *op. cit.,* p. 76.
[16] Max Scheler, *The Nature of Sympathy* (New Haven: Yale University Press, 1954), p. 142.

is a reaction to, or affected by, their sufferings, rather than a spontaneous act of *Agape*. Consequently, Bultmann believes that sympathy is not based on *Agape* but based on *Eros:* "In reality the love which is based on emotions of sympathy, on affection, is self-love; for it is a love of preference, of choice, and the standard of choice, and the standard of the preference and choice is the self."[17] Thus, the reactionary character of sympathy, which is based on the standard of preference and choice, is contrary to the very nature of *Agape,* which is spontaneous and indifferent to the value of the beloved. Furthermore, sympathy is an emotional identification through a process of imagination, which is not creative. Thus, when we are in trouble that really is not sympathy.[18] Sympathy, as an imaginary identification is, then, incompatible with the idea of *Agape,* which creates value for the worthless and lovableness for the unlovable. Finally, the concept of sympathy as the identification of oneself with the feeling of others cannot be applied to God, because God never identifies Himself except with truth and grace. *Agape* is more than a mere emotional identification through a process of imagination. It is "the drive toward the reunion of the separated"[19] through a living participation in life as a whole in order to manifest a new creation. Thus the sympathy of God as the criterion for the ascription of divine passibility is incompatible with the concept of *Agape,* which is very essence of God Himself. As a result, we suggest the empathy of God as the alternative in the approach to the problem of divine passibility.

Before examining the compatibility of the empathy of God with *Agape,* let us consider the biblical idea of divine and human relationship, which becomes a clue for the choice of the word "empathy" over against the word "sympathy." The biblical notion of "I-Thou" relationship, "I-Thou" within Godhead and "I-Thou" between man and God, is chiefly conceived in terms of participation rather than in terms of identification. There is first a prototype of participation in Godhead: "As thou, Father, art in me, and I in thee" (John 17:21). Especially in the Johannine writings, Jesus is not identified with the Father but is one with the Father (John 10:30) in terms of participation (John 10:38). When Philip asked Jesus, "Lord, show us the Father, and we shall be satisfied" (John 14:8), Jesus answered, "He who has seen me has seen the Father. ...Do you not believe that I am in the Father and the Father in me?" (John 14:9,10). At the end of this conversation, Jesus concludes with an emphatic

[17] Rudolf Bultmann, *Jesus and the Word,* trans. by Louise P. Smith and Erminie H. Lantero (New York: Charles Scribner's Sons, 1958), p. 118.

[18] E. L. Mascall, *Existence and Analogy: A Sequel to "He Who Is"* (London: Longmans, Green and Company, 1949), p. 142.

[19] Paul Tillich, *Systematic Theology,* Vol. III (Chicago: University of Chicago Press, 1963), p. 134.

appeal. "Believe me that I am in the Father and the Father in me" (John 14 : 11). Here again we are convinced that Jesus does not identify Himself with the Father but unites with Him in terms of participation. This prototype of participation in the inner life of God corresponds to the participation between God and man.

Our participation in God, that is, the reflection of the prototype of "I-Thou" participation in Godhead, is clearly expressed in Paul's experience of Christian life. From his Christian experience, he said, "it is no longer I who live, but Christ who lives in me" (Galatians 2 : 20). In order to share this experience with others, Paul wishes that Christ might also be formed (Galatians 4 : 19). In the Pauline writtings, believers are often pictured as the temple of living God, who dwells and lives among His people (I Corinthians 3 : 16; II Corinthians 6 : 16). The function of the Holy Spirit is to dwell within us (II Timothy 1 : 14; Romans 8 : 9). In the Johannine writings, the symbolic meanings of divine participation in our life are described in terms of Light (John 1 : 9), Life (John 11 : 25ff), Living Water (John 4 : 10ff), Bread (John 6 : 36, 48−58), and Blood (John 6 : 56). Therefore, it is quite apparent that God does not relate to us in terms of sympathic identification but in terms of empathic participation. The "I-Thou" relationship is, then, to be conceived not as the "I-Thou" encounter but as the "I-Thou" participation.

The term "empathy," which is much used in aesthetics and interpersonal psychology, goes back to Johannes Volket and Robert Vischer, who first introduced the German word *"Einfühlung."*[20] *"Einfühlung,"* which literally means "in-feeling," has its root in the reflexive verb *"sich einfühlen,"* which is commonly translated into English as "to feel oneself into." Consequently, the empathy of God means that God feels Himself into the world, that is, the participation of divine pathos in the world. Here, "feeling" and "pathos" are interchangeably used. In other words, the empathy of God is defined as the participation of divine feeling (or pathos) into human feeling that the unity of feeling (not the imaginary identity) is attained.

The "feeling that feels" or "pathos" here is used as "Prehension" in a Whiteheadian sense. In other words, "Here 'feeling' is the term used for the basic generic operation of passing from the objectivity of data to the subjectivity of the actual entity in question."[21] As a generic term "feeling" of "pathos" is complete in itself and includes the species of feeling, such as will, reason, and so forth. It is total in its activity. Thus it is similar to Bergson's use of the term

---

[20] Herbert Read, *The Forms of Things Unknown: Essays Towards an Aesthetic Philosophy* (New York: Horizon Press, 1960), p. 87.

[21] Alfred North Whitehead, *Process and Creativity* (New York: The Macmillan Company, 1929), p. 65.

"intuition."[22] Feeling or pathos is then the "vector" of experience.[23] It conveys an entirety of experience, because experience is nothing but a process of feeling. Thus, everything is for feeling. Whitehead says, "Every reality is there for feeling: it promotes feeling; and it is felt."[24] Feeling or pathos is then the "vector" of entire experience that one experiences in participation. Thus, empathy as the participation of feeling or "in-feeling" (or "*em*-pathy") means to *experience* the total self. In other words, the meaning of the divine empathy as the participation of divine feeling or pathos into human feeling is none other than the unity of the divine and human experience in its complete sense. The unity of experience between God and man is, then, possible through the empathy of God. God and man are united and become one in *experience*. Thus, the empathy of God makes Him Possible to be united with man in experience. This unity of experience through the unity of feeling is possible only in participation. This is precisely why the empathy of God is differentiated from the sympathy of God. It is not the identification of divine pathos but the participation of it into the world that makes the unity of experience between man and God possible. In this participation the experience of God is united with the experience of man. It is not the merger of God and man; but the unity of them is possible because of the unity of their experience in empathy. Thus, in the empathy of God, God fully participates in us as the Person without losing His essential nature as the divine, so that we can also participate in His participation as persons without losing our essential nature as a human being. Therefore, this genuine personal relationship between God and man (or the "I-Thou" participation) is possible because of divine empathy.

Unlike the sympathy of God, the empathy of God is the way of *Agape*. Johannine literature illustrates this with distinctive clarity: "If we love one another, God abides in us and His love is perfected in us" (I John 4 : 12). We abide in Him by His love (John 15 : 9,10). Since *Agape* leads us neither to identify ourselves with God nor God with us, the empathy of God makes neither us to be in God's place without Him nor God in our place without us. *Agape* does not make us to be like God but us to be united with Him in our experience in terms of empathy. In this respect, the empathy of God is nothing else than a functional mode of *Agape*. In other words, *Agape* is the basis of divine empathy, while the empathy of God is a mode of *Agape*. The empathy of God is a way of *Agape,* the way toward the dialectical union experience between the divine and the human being who is constantly

---

[22]   *Ibid.*
[23]   *Ibid.,* p. 133.
[24]   *Ibid.,* p. 472.

alienating himself from the presence of the divine. In this unifying act of experience, the nature of God as "He-is-in-Himself" becomes God as "He-is-for-us" of *Agape*. In empathy of God, God is always for us, because it is the way of His love. However, man is not always in God. Man as a sinner revolts against God's participation in him. This revolt of man creates in God the inner tension which is analogous with a form of frustration. It is the very nature of God to love through participation of His pathos, but His participation is denied. Without participation God's love is not possible. Man's sin builds a wall around him, so that God's participation is denied. The denial of participation is the denial of love. The love that is denied to participate in the beloved is the estranged love, the suffering love. If God is love, the suffering love is certainly a suffering God.

An Application of the Criterion: The Meaning of Divine Passibility

We now come to the heart of our question, that is, the suffering of God itself. As we said, the empathy of God or the participation of divine pathos in the sinful world of man creates in Him the inner tension which is characterized as His suffering. This inner tension of God is manifested in divine wrath, which represents the symbol of the action of God's estranged love.

Before we discuss the concept of divine wrath as a symbolic manifestation of God's inner tension, we may consider a little further the nature of this tension. This inner tension, which is created by the empathy of God, presupposes two basic assumptions: the dialectical unity between transcendence and immanence in *Agape,* and the sin of man which represents existential estrangement. As we have already made clear, in the essential nature of *Agape* there is the dialectical unity between the transcendental character which corresponds to the holiness and righteousness of God, and the immanental character which corresponds to the mercy and grace of God. This unity is paradoxical in nature, because there is a harmonious co-existence in spite of the sharp and essential contrast between transcendence and immanence. Transcendence creates distance, but immanence creates communion. Transcendence erects barriers, but immanence breaks through them. Transcendence rejects sin, and immanence overcomes it. The transcendence of God represents the eternal will to assert His own glory and power, while the immanence of God symbolizes the compassionate heart to renounce and sacrifice Himself in the world. Nevertheless, both of them are paradoxically united in *Agape*. They are united not in terms of mergence but in terms of a mutual inclusiveness. In other words, "Immanence is not transcendence, yet it is the transcendent that is immanent."[25] *Agape* is, then, neither the divine transcendence without divine immanence nor the divine immanence without divine transcendence, but the inclusive unity of them. Therefore, we assume that in *Agape* the paradoxical unity between transcendence and immanence is essentially preserved in harmony.

In the empathy of God the harmony is threatened because of sin, which represents the power of disharmony and estrangement. This threat produces an acute tension within the inner life of divine love. This strained tension between transcendence and immanence in *Agape*, which is created by the empathy of God on account of sin and evil, is the conflict of movements due to the dialectic dualism which is inherited in the essential nature of the divine. To be brief, the potential conflict of movements between transcendence and immanence in *Agape* is actualized in the empathy of God because of sin and evil. When *Agape* is concretely involved in the existential estrangement, that is, the state of man's self-alienation from the ground of his being,[26] the divine transcendence rejects its participation in the state of being estranged, while the divine immanence moves into that state to transform it. This conflict of movements which is due to the empathy of God (participation of divine pathos in human feeling to have the unity of experience) is a creative tension, because this dialectic tension alone is able to achieve the redemptive process. The redemption begins with the judgment of sin and ends with the transformation of it. The former is primarily the function of divine transcendence, while the latter is that of divine immanence. However, the activity of divine transcendence always presupposes that of divine immanence, while the activity of divine immanence is always fulfilled by that of divine transcendence. Thus the redemptive process of God implies the creative struggle between transcendence and immanence in *Agape*. "This leads to," what Tillich calls, "the fundamental assertion: the divine life is the eternal conquest of the negative."[27]

The nature of this dialectical tension in the inner life of the divine is clearly manifested in the Scripture as the wrath of God. The wrath of God is, therefore, to be understood as an act of the inner struggle between the transcendence and immanence of God when He is fully involved in the existential estrangement of the world. It is a symbol of the struggling love of God to accept that which is also rejected by Him. Thus the wrath of God is neither

[25] H. Maurice Relton, *Studies in Christian Doctrine* (London: The Macmillan Company, 1960), p. 57.
[26] Paul Tillich, *Systematic Theology*, Vol. II (Chicago: University of Chicago Press, 1957), 44 ff.
[27] Tillich, *Systematic Theology, III*, 405.

something alien to the love of God nor a counterpole of it, but simply the love of God in conflict. Albert Knudson calls it "a restrained manifestation of love"[28] occasioned by our sin. The divine wrath is the manifestation of God's estranged love because of man's sin.

In the Old Testament the concept of divine wrath is manifest toward Israelites who violate the covenant (Leviticus 10 : 6; Numbers 16 : 46; Psalms 78 : 31). It is often associated with the Day of Judgment (Isaiah 2 : 10−22; Jeremiah 30 : 7ff). The wrath of God is, then, accompanied with divine judgment upon the sin of man. This idea is also expressed in the New Testament. According to Paul, the wrath of God reveals the ungodliness and wickedness of man (Romans 1 : 18). For all are in the state of estrangement; all mankind is the object of divine wrath (Romans 3 : 9−18). Thus the wrath of God implies His uncompromising denial of sin, in spite of His eternal love to participate in His children's lives. This divine disposition against evil is manifest only for a moment in comparison with eternal love, for the wrath of God is implicit in the love of God. "In overflowing wrath for a moment I hide my face from you, but with everlasting love I will have compassion on you, says the Lord, your Redeemer" (Isaiah 54 : 8−10). God is also "slow to anger," because He is "abounding in steadfast love" (Psalms 103 : 8). And "He does not retain his anger forever because he delights in steadfast love" (Micah 7 : 18). The wrath of God is, therefore, characterized as "suspended love" or "mercy withheld,"[29] so that man may allow God to empathize in him. In other words, it can be understood as the impatience of *Agape,* which occasions us to participate in the empathy of God. The impatience of *Agape* means that the harmonious coexistence of divine transcendence and immanence is disturbed by the persistent rebellion of sin. Therefore, the wrath of God is a biblical symbol which describes the restrained mode of *Agape,* or the empathy of God unrealized.

Until now we have made an attempt to demonstrate that there is an inevitable tension between divine transcendence and immanence within the life of God as a result of the empathy of God in our sinful existence. Let us now examine whether or not this inner tension of God corresponds to a concept of divine suffering. In order to do this, we may begin our examination with a clear understanding of the meaning of suffering which we attribute to the divine.

Since the word "suffering" is often indiscriminately used with the word

---

[28]   Albert C. Knudson, *The Doctrine of God* (New York: The Abingdon Press, 1930), p. 347.
[29]   Abraham J. Heschel, *The Prophets* (New York: Harper and Row, 1966), p. 295.

"pain,"[30] a clear distinction between these two words may help us in our attempt to ascribe a concept of suffering to the divine. Pain is bound to the body which puts us in touch with things. "This explains why contemporary philosophers are almost unanimously inclined to consider pain as a sensation which depends upon some exterior stimulus such as visual or auditory sensation."[31] On the other hand, suffering is much more complex. "In reality, we suffer only in our relations with others."[32] Suffering occurs when the bonds which relate us to others are threatened or destroyed. "Suffering deals with the inward disposition of man, while pain deals with the bodily sensation of man."[33] Suffering deals with psychological and spiritual dimensions of life even though it is inseparable with pain, which deals with the physical dimension of life. The intensity of suffering is, then, to be measured by the intimacy of the relationship with whom love is directed. This is why we do not suffer with those who are indifferent to us. On the other hand, the possibility of pain is measured by the seriousness of the exterior stimulus of sensation. Thus, pain rightly belongs to the sphere of bio-physiological study. However, in our human life both suffering and pain are so intimately associated with each other that we cannot have one without the other. A psychosomatic disease is one good example that illustrates the close association between suffering and pain in our lives. The psychosomatic disease can be understood as the transitional process of suffering to pain, that is, the transition of psychic and interpersonal disorders to biological and physiological malformations in a human body. As the spirit and body are united in a human entity, the experience of suffering and pain are intimately united in each other.

However, when we speak of divine experience, we cannot apply the concept of pain. Since God is Spirit, the category of pain, which we have understood in terms of a sensation bound to the physical body, does not belong to Him. Therefore, the concept of suffering is a legitimate form only of divine experience.

If we understand suffering in terms of the loving relationship, in every form of loving relationship there must be at least the potentiality of suffering. This is to say that the relationship of love is a potential form of suffering. A risk for suffering exists when we love others. This risk is also apparent in God's loving relation to the world. The potentiality of suffering increases in

---

[30] Some of the good examples of the discriminate use of the words "pain" and "suffering" are found in Kitamori's *Theology of the Pain of God*, and Woollcombe's article "The Pain of God" in *The Scottish Journal of Theology* (June, 1967).

[31] Louis Lavelle, *Evil and Suffering*, trans. by Bernard Murchland (New York: The Macmillan Company, 1963), p. 64.

[32] *Ibid.*, p. 65.

[33] Jung Young Lee, *The I: A Christian Concept of Man* (New York: Philosophical Library, 1971), p. 61.

proportion to the intensity of loving relationship. At the same time, the potentiality of divine suffering is to be understood in terms of the intimacy of His love which works through His empathy, the participation of His pathos. Likewise, the potentiality of our Christian suffering is measured in terms of the depth of the Christian love. This is why those who are afraid of suffering are unable to love God or others, because in every form of loving relationship there is a risk of suffering. Thus Kierkegaard calls suffering "the distinguishing mark of religious action,"[34] for "this suffering means the relationship,"[35] the relationship of love.

How, then, does this potential form of suffering actualize itself in our relationship with others? Suffering is actually experienced when the possible or actual threat of destruction exists in our loving relationship. The possible threat of this destruction is by and large based on our mistrust and unbelief in whom we love. Thus the man of unbelief is always in danger of suffering in spite of his love. However, the actual suffering takes place whenever there is the destruction or estrangement of loving relationship. The destruction of that relationship may produce the most severe suffering, which we often experience when our closest one leaves us alone by death or by separation.

The estrangement of loving relationship also produces the actual experience of suffering, which is due to the lack of harmony. This kind of suffering can be most creative and constructive if a meaning and purpose are found in it. The concept of suffering which can attribute to the divine ought to be this kind of suffering, because God's loving relationship with the world through the empathy of God cannot be destroyed by the evil force of the world. The loving relationship between God and the world, which is established by the empathy of God, is not destroyed but distorted by the estrangement of human existence. However, we must make clear that it is not the power of our sin to distort this relationship, but it is God's way of response to the sin of man whom He loves. It is the transcendental character of love which rejects us on account of our sins, while it is the immanental character of love which accepts us on account of His children. This inner disharmony of divine transcendence and immanence in *Agape* becomes the prototype of all other distortions of our relationship with God.

In attributing suffering to the divine, our primary interest is in the prototype of estrangement which takes place within the inner life of God. Since "suffering is the highest action in inwardness,"[36] any experience of suffering which

---

[34] Søren Kierkegaard, *Concluding Unscientific Postscript,* trans. by David F. Swenson (Princeton: Princeton University Press, 1941), p. 387.
[35] *Ibid.,* p. 405.
[36] *Ibid.,* p. 388.

is not an inward activity cannot be the actual suffering. Suffering may be due to a loving relationship which is external to our entity, but the real experience of suffering is an activity in our inwardness. Even though God's suffering is a consequence of our sin which is external to Him, the actual experience of His suffering takes place within the inner life of Himself. Thus, the inner tension between the divine transcendence and immanence in *Agape* seems to correspond with the idea of suffering as an inward activity. In other words, the passibility of God may imply that there is the possibility of disharmony and disturbance of transcendence and immanence in *Agape* by the empathy of God due to the sins of the world. The impassibility of God means, on the other hand, "His own inner happiness is not disturbed."[37] Since the inner disharmony in *Agape* corresponds to the suffering as an inward experience, we are readily convinced to affirm that God as *Agape* is passible. That is to say that the God whose nature is *Agape* is capable of suffering.

However, we must make clear that the very nature of *Agape* is not suffering but is capable only for suffering. Since *Agape* has the potential of suffering, it is closely related with redemptive suffering itself. Love is only *Agape* insofar as it is able to suffer, and the suffering of God is only vicarious and redemptive suffering as it is rooted in *Agape.* Love without a capacity of suffering is not *Agape,* and suffering without the motive of love is not divine suffering. Love is the fulfillment of suffering, and suffering is the enduring strength of love. Suffering is subsequent to love, and love is carried out by suffering. These two do not stand side by side and separate from one another, but united together. Even though they are united, they are not identical. Love is able to suffer, but it never suffers by itself. *Agape,* then, suffers only in relation to what is being estranged from God. In other words, *Agape* suffers *only* in the empathy of God on account of the sin of the world. That is, God suffers only in the participation of His pathos in the world of sin. Thus the passibility of God actualizes itself in the empathy of God. Since God's suffering is actualized by the empathy of God, these three—love, suffering and empathy—are united in the redemptive work of God. Love directs the course of divine movement, empathy connects the movement of the world, and suffering endures the sinful rebellion of the world for redemption. Since they are inseparably united together in divine life, we cannot say that *Agape* is redemptive suffering without the empathy of God. Thus God as *Agape* suffers only in His empathy. For this reason, the empathy of God becomes the criterion for the ascription of a concept of suffering to God.

If God as *Agape* suffers in His empathy in the world, what would the nature

---

[37] Peter Anthony Bertocci, *An Introduction to the Philosophy of Religion* (Englewood Cliffs, New Jersey: Prentice-Hall, Incorporated, 1951), p. 458.

of His suffering be like? Even though the nature of divine suffering is mystery to us, we are led to believe that there is a possibility of discerning an analogous knowledge about it. The analogous knowledge is given to us in the biblical symbol which depicts the nature of divine suffering. Just as the wrath of God is the symbol of the manifestation of divine inner tension, the "Servant of the Lord" is a characteristic symbol of divine suffering. The concept of the "Servant of the Lord" is vividly described in Deutero-Isaiah, particularly in Isaiah 42 : 1–4; 49 : 1–6; 50 : 4–9; and 52 : 13–53 : 12. We are not going to speculate who the suffering servant is,[38] whether he represents an individual or the community of Israel. Whatever exegetical theories we may uphold, the "Servant of the Lord" can be taken as a symbol of divine suffering, which becomes an historical reality in the suffering of Jesus Christ (Matthew 12 : 18–21; Acts 3 : 13). A clear evidence that Jesus thought of His sufferings as having been "written of him" (Matthew 26 : 24, 54, 56) signifies that the suffering of the "Servant of the Lord" corresponds to the suffering of God in Jesus Christ. It is in this respect that Kitamori also regards the suffering of the "Servant of the Lord as the symbol of divine suffering."[39]

Our special attention is to be given to the last servant poem in Deutero-Isaiah 52 : 13–53 : 12, which seems to depict plainly the characteristics of divine suffering. When we examine this poem carefully, we first notice that the servant suffers with deep humiliation. "The suffering servant has appeared among them *incognito,* unrecognized in his disguise of humiliation."[40] He who suffers with humiliation is illustrated as the one who has "no form or come-liness that we should look at him, and no beauty that we should desire him" (Isaiah 53 : 2). Moreover, "He was despised and rejected by men; a man of sorrows, and acquainted with grief; and as one from whom men hide their faces he was despised, and we esteemed him not" (Isaiah 53 : 3). The suffering of the humiliated God is well expressed by Bonhoeffer. In his letter from prison he writes, "Men go to God in his need, find him poor, scorned, without shelter and bread, see him consumed by sin, weakness and death."[41]

Secondly, divine suffering with humiliation is the hardest and greatest. The worst of all sufferings was experienced by the "Servant of the Lord," who was despised and rejected (Isaiah 53 : 8), and "cut off out of the land of the living" (Isaiah 53 : 8). Loneliness and humiliation are the most bitter afflic-

---

[38] In identifying the "Servant of the Lord" there are mainly four theories: "The Servant is 1) an anonymous contemporary of Second Isaiah; 2) Second Isaiah himself; 3) Israel; 4) a purely ideal or imaginary figure." See Heschel, *op. cit.,* p. 149.

[39] Kitamori, *op. cit.,* p. 62.

[40] Bernhard W. Anderson, *Understanding the Old Testament* (Englewood Cliffs, New Jersey: Prentice-Hall, Incorporated, 1957), p. 424.

[41] J. Robert Nelson, "Tolerance, Bigotry, and the Christian Faith," *Religion in Life* (Autumn, 1964), p. 556. See also Bonhoeffer, *Prisoner for God,* p. 167.

tions to the Oriental. For example, "Cain's grievous punishment is that he is exiled from community."[42] Since the intensity of suffering is proportionate to the intimacy of relationship, the God who relates Himself unconditionally to love the world is the greatest sufferer of all. In other words, "If God's love be infinite, then He can suffer infinitely too."[43] The suffering of God is immeasurably greater than ours because of His all-participating and all-comprehending love.

Thirdly, the suffering of God is vicarious and self-giving. The greatest suffering which He bears with shame and humiliation is not for His own but for the sake of our sins. He freely bears the burden of our iniquities, because we have gone astray and turned away from His presence (Isaiah 53 : 6). That is why "he was wounded for our transgressions, he was bruised for our iniquities" (Isaiah 53 : 5). Moreover, the servant himself becomes an offering for our guilt (Isaiah 53 : 10), as though Christ has offered Himself for the penalty for our sins. Therefore, the vicarious suffering which we understand in the Bible is an act of grace, "and grace here means the voluntary acceptance of the suffering in the working out of the divine purpose to save."[44]

Fimally, the nature of divine suffering which we can analogize in the "Servant of the Lord" is a redemptive act. The redemptive act of God is in itself the vicarious suffering of God in the world. In this respect, the song of the "Servant of the Lord" exalts the suffering servant as an agent of divine blessings for many.

... When he makes himself an offering for sin, he shall see his offspring, he shall prolong his days; the will of the Lord shall prosper in his hand; he shall see the fruit of the travail of his soul and be satisfied; by his knowledge shall the righteous one, my servant, make many to be accounted righteous; and he shall bear their iniquities (Isaiah 53 : 10, 11).

Since this vicarious suffering of the servant represents the redemptive act of God in the world, "the height and depth of God" is revealed "in this form of His suffering."[45] Therefore, the nature of divine suffering is to be understood not in terms of *patheia,* which is inert and defective, but in terms of *agonia,* which is creative and redemptive.

To sum up, the nature of divine suffering, which is symbolized in the "Servant of the Lord" as a whole, is the hardest and greatest suffering with

---

[42] James Muilenburg, "The Book of Isaiah, Chapters 40–66," *Interpreter's Bible,* Vol. V, edited by George Arthur Buttrick (New York: The Abingdon Press, 1956), p. 620.

[43] J. K. Mozley, *The Impassibility of God: A Survey of Christian Thought* (Cambridge: University Press, 1926), p. 151.

[44] H. Wheeler Robinson, *Suffering, Human and Divine* (New York: The Macmillan Company, 1939), p. 182.

[45] Barth, *Church Dogmatics, IV/3,* 420.

deep humiliation, a vicarious sacrifice, and creative energy for the redemption of the world. It seems appropriate to conclude this chapter with a profound insight of Bonhoeffer, whose keen sensitivity could perceive so vividly the characteristics of divine suffering as revealed in Jesus Christ.

... It is infinitely easier to suffer in obedience to a human command than to suffer in the freedom of an act undertaken purely on one's own responsibility. It is infinitely easier to suffer in community than to suffer in loneliness. It is infinitely easier to suffer openly and in honour than to suffer apart and in shame. It is infinitely easier to suffer by risking one's physical life than to suffer in spirit. Christ suffered in freedom, in loneliness, apart and in shame, in body and in spirit, and many Christians have since suffered with him.[46]

---

[46] H. Gollwitzer, et al. (ed.), Dying We Live: The Final Messages and Records of Some Germans Who Defied Hitler, trans. by Reinhard C. Kuhn (London: Harvill Press, 1956), p. 171.

CHAPTER II

THE NEGATION OF DIVINE PASSIBILITY:
AN EXAMINATION OF A TRADITIONAL
DOCTRINE OF DIVINE IMPASSIBILITY

In the previous chapter we defined a concept of divine passibility in terms of the empathy of God. In order to do this, we first considered the importance of distinguishing between the nature and attribute of God, because the attribute is always conditioned by the nature. Since we have concluded that *Agape* is the nature of God, we have made an attempt to postulate a concept of divine passibility as a divine attribute on the basis of *Agape*. We have also made a distinction between what God is in Himself and what God is in us. If *Agape* is the nature of God, it must represent both what God is and what God does. As the attribute is conditioned by the nature, the attributive aspect of *Agape*, that is, what God does, is effected by the very nature of *Agape,* that is, what God is. What God is in Himself becomes what God is in us. This act of love works in us in terms of the empathy of God. We have defined the empathy of God as the participation of divine pathos or feeling in human feeling, which unites both divine and human experience. Thus, the participation of divine pathos or the empathy of God is in the unity of *experience* which makes the unity of being possible. In this empathy the dialectical harmony of divine transcendence with divine immanence in *Agape* is disturbed on account of our sinful existence in the world. This inner disturbance of God is attributed to our understanding of divine suffering. The transition of the harmony to the disharmony of *Agape* takes place not because of the sympathy of God but because of the empathy of God. Therefore, it is not the sympathy but the empathy of God which becomes the criterion for the ascription of a concept of suffering to the divine.

We now come to apply this criterion to examine whether a traditional understanding of divine impassibility is valid or not. As a matter of procedure, we may begin with a clear analysis of basic assumptions for the assertion of a doctrine of divine impassibility. We may then consider some of the serious objections to the ascription of a concept of divine passibility. We may end with an examination of these assumptions and objections in the light of the empathy of God.

The Basic Assumptions for the Assertion
of Divine Impassibility

For the purpose of ascertaining the basic assumptions for the assertion of divine impassibility, we may begin with this question: "What were the fundamental issues in the early Church to affirm the doctrine of divine impassibility?" One of the basic issues which brought the problem of divine passibility was the question of the Trinity. The trinitarian issue was directly related to the affirmation of the doctrine of divine impassibility by the early Church. In addition to this theological issue, we cannot overlook the importance of Greek philosophy which became the background of theological thinking in the early and medieval church Fathers in general. The significant contributions of Greek philosophy to the formation of the doctrine of divine impassibility might be summarized as follows: the concept of apathy as the supreme moral task, and the concept of ontological immutability. If we summarize what we have said so far, we may safely presume that the basic assumptions for the assertion of the doctrine of divine impassibility are primarily three: the distinctions of "persons" in the Trinity, the Greek idea of divine apathy, and the static notion of divine sufficiency. We may consider them separately in order to see the significance of their places in the origin of the doctrine.

1. The Distinctions of "Persons" in the Trinity

Even though it is not our intention to survey the historical development of the doctrine of divine impassibility, we cannot neglect the historical significance of this doctrine. The origin of the patripassian heresy, which was the most pronounced name in the early Church for the passibility of God, was closely connected with the problem of the Trinity. In other words, "Patripassianism is directly come from trinitarian issue, the Sabellianism, from which patripassianism is logically deduced, since there is only a difference in name."[1] Thus, those who rejected the distinctions of "persons" in the Trinity were called "Patripassians" in the West and "Sabellians" in the East. [2] The origin of the name "Patripassian" is in the combination of two Latin words: *Pater* (father) and *passio* (suffering). It meant that God the Father Himself suffered. This idea was based on the christological and trinitarian thinking that the Father, Son and the Holy Spirit were regarded in the unity of one Person. Thus, Modalistic Monarchianism, which insisted upon the unity of Godhead through the identification of the Son with the Father, was first called by Tertullian "Patripassianism."[3] "Patripassianism" was, then, a nickname for "Modalistic Monarchianism," which was commonly

[1] John L. Murphy, *The General Councils of the Church* (Milwaukee: Bruce Publishing Company, 1960), p. 19.

[2] Marshall Randles, *The Blessed God, Impassibility* (London: Charles H. Kelly, 1900), p. 16.

[3] The prevalent term, "patripassians," may be traced to Tertullian *(Adversus Praxean)*. See Reinhold Seeberg, *The Textbook of the History of Christian Doctrines*, trans. by Charles E. Hay, Vol. I (Grand Rapids: Baker Book House, 1964), 166.

associated with "Sabellianism." Thus these three were often used synonymously to designate the same movement. Patripassian monarchianism was associated especially with the names of Praxeas and Noetus in the early stage of its development and Zephrinus and Callistus of Rome in the later stage.

Our chief source of information concerning Praxeas is Tertullian's treatise, *Adversus Praxean,* which has become an important work of Western theology on the Trinity before the time of Augustine. From this source we come to recognize that Praxeas, a martyr of Asia Minor, came to Rome in order to influence the Bishop of Rome to "acknowledge the prophetic gifts of Montanus, Priscilla, and Maximilla, and in consequence of the acknowledgement had bestowed his peace on the churches of Asia and Phrygia."[4] As a result, Praxeas had done "two pieces of the devil's work in Rome: he drove out prophecy and he brought in heresy; he put to flight the paraclete and he crucified the Father."[5] This new heresy, which was vigorously attacked by Tertullian as Patripassian, seemed to have its origin in Praxeas' anxiety to maintain the unity of God, which, he thought, could only be done by identifying the Father, Son and Holy Spirit together as one and the same. Because Praxeas failed to make the distinction between the persons in Godhead, "he says that the Father Himself came down into the virgin, was Himself born of her, Himself suffered, indeed was Himself Jesus Christ."[6] Moreover, on this principle Tertullian accused him of implying the death of the Father:

"We are not guilty of blasphemy," says Tertullian, "against the Lord God, for we do not maintain that He died after the divine nature, but only after the human. Nay, but you do blaspheme; because you allege not only that the Father died, but that He died the death of the Cross."[7]

Thus it is quite clear that Praxeas' failure to maintain the distinctions between the "persons" in the Trinity resulted in the patripassian heresy.

Another name which was closely associated with the Patripassian heresy was Noetus, who was mainly known to us through the writings of Hippolytus. Like Praxeas, Noetus, who was born in Smyrna, introduced the Modalistic heresy in the Church. Noetus also affirmed that the Father and the Son are the same and one. This idea was clearly illustrated in his own statement as follows:

... "When, indeed, at the time the Father was not yet born, He was justly styled the Father; and when it pleased Him to undergo generation and to be begotten, He Him-

---

[4] Tertullian, *Adversus Praxean,* Chapter I.
[5] *Ibid.*
[6] *Ibid.*
[7] *Ibid.,* Chapter 29.

self became His own Son, not another's." For in this manner he thinks he establishes the Monarcy, alleging that the Father and the Son, so called, are not from one another, but one and the same, Himself from Himself, and that He is styled by the names Father and Son, according to the changes of times.[8]

Noetus' modalistic assertion of Godhead was eventually accused of teaching that the Father Himself suffered and died on the Cross. Over against this heretical assertion, Hippolytus defended a concept of anti-patripassianism on the basis of the economy of Trinity. Hippolytus was dissatisfied with Noetus' justification that the Modalistic concept of God was based on the saying of Jesus that "I and the Father are one." Hippolytus' argument was that Jesus did not say that "I and the Father *am* one, but *are* one." Since the word "are" was not said of one person and referred to two persons in one power, the Father and the Son ought to be differentiated.[9] In this way Hippolytus was successful in defeating the patripassian movement in his time. Again, the patripassian heresy of Noetus was a result of his failure to make the distinctions of "persons" in the Trinity.[10]

According to Hippolytus, both Zephyrinus and Callistus of Rome were influenced by Noetus.[11] Zephyrinus was incompetent and unskilled in ecclesiastical definitions, even though he was the Bishop of Rome at that time. It was, therefore, his advisor Callistus who influenced him to act similarly toward those who followed the teaching of Sabellius.[12] In other words, Callistus

... induced him (Zephyrinus) to avow publicly the following opinions: "I know that there is one God, Jesus Christ; nor accept Him do I know any other that is begotten and susceptible to suffering." On another occasion he made the following statement: "The Father did not die, but the Son." Zephyrinus would in this way continue to keep up ceaseless disturbance among the people.[13]

Consequently, Zephyrinus was confused and unable to commit himself to any definite position. Since Callistus committed himself more definitely to

---

[8]   Hippolytus, *Refutatio*, II.
[9]   Hippolytus, "Against the Heresy of One Noetus," *Ante-Nicene Fathers: Translations of the Writings of the Fathers Down to A.D. 325,* Vol. V, edited by Alexander Roberts and James Donaldson (Grand Rapids: Wm. B. Eerdmans Publishing Company, 1957), p. 7.
[10]   However, "in some sense Noetus did try to draw a distinction between the terms "Father" and "Son . . . . he draws a distinction between the One God before and after the Incarnation." See H. M. Relton, *Studies in Christian Doctrine* (New York: The Macmillan Company, 1960), p. 69. Nevertheless, in incarnation the Father and the Son are regarded as identical, and in this sense both of them suffer and die together.
[11]   Hippolytus, *Refutatio*, IX, 7.
[12]   *Ibid.,* IX, 11, 1.
[13]   *Ibid.,* IX, 11, 3.

what was so-called the modified form of patripassian heresy, we had better consider his teaching as the representation of Zephyrinus' opinion.

After the death of Zephyrinus, Callistus succeeded him as the Bishop of Rome. As soon as he became the Bishop of Rome, he attacked both Sabellius and Hippolytus. He first "excommunicated Sabellius, as not entertaining right opinions."[14] He then accused Hippolytus and his followers of being "Ditheists."[15] As a result, he was blamed by both Sabellius, who frequently accused him of transgressing his first faith, and Hippolytus, who called him an imposter. To be rescued from this ideological turmoil, Callistus decided to advocate a somewhat modified form of monarchianistic christology, even though he denied the agreement with Sabellius, for the sake of consistency. He emphasized the unity of Godhead in the Spirit: "The Spirit, which became incarnate in the virgin, is not different from the Father, but one and the same."[16] Thus he claimed that the Father did not suffer as the Son, but "the Father suffered *with* the Son."[17] In this way he attempted to avoid any blasphemy against God the Father. However, this compromising formula of Callistus did not prevent him from being accused of following the practice of Praxeas and Noetus.

Tertullian also dealt with the modified form of Modalism, although he did not mention the name of Callistus in this connection in his treatise on *Adversus Praxean,* especially in Chapters 27 and 29. Tertullian fought against any compromising statement, that is, the co-passion of the Father, as he rejected the earlier form of Modalism ascribed by Praxeas and Noetus. It was the consistent claim of Tertullian that God as the Father was incapable of suffering. His uncompromising position was well illustrated in his statement as follows:

... "For what is the meaning of 'fellow-suffering,'" said Tertullian, "but the endurance of suffering along with other? Now if the Father is incapable of suffering, He is incapable of suffering in company with another; otherwise, if He can suffer with another, He is of course capable of suffering."[18]

Tertullian's argument of anti-patripassianism was based on the idea that the divine nature was completely free from any form of suffering by drawing the sharp distinction between the divine and human nature in Christ. Therefore, there was no room in his trinitarian thinking for the doctrine of compassion or co-passion, namely Father suffering with the Son. Later, "The Church,"

---

14   *Ibid.,* IX, 12, 15.
15   *Ibid.,* IX, 12, 16.
16   *Ibid.,* IX, 12, 17.
17   *Ibid.,* IX, 12, 18.
18   Tertullian, *op. cit.,* Chapter 29.

following the line of his thinking, "made distinctions [of divine persons in the Trinity], which were intended to be a safeguard against any ascription of passibility to the divine nature."[19] We, therefore, conclude that it was the distinctions of "persons" in the Trinity which became not only the fundamental motive but the basic assumption for the assertion of the anti-patripassian doctrine in the early Church.

2. *The Greek Idea of Divine Apatheia*

In the previous section we have attempted to support the thesis that the fundamental motive for the assertion of divine impassibility was primarily based on the struggle to safeguard the distinctions of "persons" in the Trinity against Patripassian Monarchianism in the early Church. This was the theological issue which was directly associated with the formation of the doctrine of divine impassibility. There was also a philosophical issue which was indirectly related to the affirmation of this doctrine. This was the Greek mode of thinking about the divine nature. Since Christianity grew up in the world of Hellenistic culture, it was predominately the Greek philosophy which became the background of religious thinking. We presume that there were two specific aspects of the Greek way of thinking, namely the concept of divine *apatheia* and *autarkeia,* which nourished the idea of divine impassibility. Thus, let us first begin our examination with the Greek idea of divine *apatheia.*

Divine *apatheia* means simply that there is an absence of feeling or passion in the divine nature. It implies, in other words, that God is free of any emotional life. According to the Greek way of thinking in general, the divine is regarded as the perfection of the Good, which can only be contemplated by the rational faculty and not by passion or feeling. One of the characteristics of Greek philosophy is the degradation of passion. Thus God, who is the Good, cannot be considered to possess the element of passion or feeling in His own nature. God is, then, unable to suffer or to feel, as a human being does. This idea of divine apathy can be traced back to the teachings of Plato, Aristotle, the Stoics and the Neoplatonists.

In Plato's philsophy there is an almost dualistic notion of reason and emotion. Reason is a faculty which moves upward to the divine, while passion is that which pulls downward to the contamination of the flesh. In *The Republic* Plato illustrates this dichotomy in terms of archery: "It is like an archer

---

[19] J. K. Mozley, *The Impassability of God: A Survey of Christian Thought* (Cambridge: University Press, 1926), p. 127.

drawing the bow: it is not accurate to say that his hands are at the same time both pushing and pulling it. One hand does the pushing, the other the pulling."[20] The hand which pushes toward the Good represents the rational faculty, and that which pulls down signifies the emotional aspect of man. The element of passion represents not only an irrational nature of man but an inclination toward the lesser good. Thus Plato associates passion with an animal instinct of man, which is rather commonly observed in the behavior of children.[21] Consequently, the divine who represents the perfection of the highest good must be free from any element of pathos.

Aristotle takes a somewhat modified view of the relationship between passion and reason. Even though he teaches the unity of human soul, he still places the rational faculty above passion or feeling. He asks us to restrain desire and emotion through the exercise of reason.[22] However, we must not be ashamed of having passion or feeling, since it belongs to our own nature. Even though "it is difficult to rub off this passion,"[23] we must attempt to control and restrain according to reason. In this respect, passion or feeling never takes an important place in the human soul.

The Platonic notion of reason and passion dichotomy has been radically reasserted by the Stoics, who believe that the human soul is divided into two different compartments. By analogy reason dwells "upstairs," and passion resides "downstairs." In other words, the Stoics make a sharp contrast between reason and passion. For them passion or emotion represents "unreasoned impulse" and "a false judgment." It is in itself "a moral evil."[24] Reason, on the other hand, is highly exalted. Reason belongs to the divine nature in man, while passion to the animal nature in him. It is the power of reason which can only bring us to the divine, since God is regarded as the Logos or the Reason, which is the source of human reason. In other words, "In dialectics we are led up to the Supreme Reason, the Logos or Word, whose divine being permeates the universe."[25] Therefore, the supreme goal of the Stoics is *apatheia,* which is exalted beyond all other aspects of life.

The Platonic concept of the hierarchy of good is reinterpreted by Plotinus in terms of a divine emanation. In the divine emanation reason is regarded as

[20] Plato, *The Republic of Plato,* trans. by F. M. Cornford (Oxford: The Clarendon Press, 1941), p. 133.

[21] *Ibid.,* p. 135.

[22] Aristotle, *Ethica Nicomachea,* edited by W. D. Ross (Oxford: The Clarendon Press, 1925), 1108a.

[23] *Ibid.,* 1105a.

[24] E. Vernon Arnold, *Roman Stoicism: Being Lectures on the History of the Stoic Philosophy with Special Reference to its Development within the Roman Empire* (New York: The Humanities Press, 1958), p. 352.

[25] R. M. Wenley, *Stoicism and Its Influence* (London: Longmans, Green and Company, 1927), pp. 218–219.

the proper activity of the World-Soul. According to Plotinus' metaphysical scheme, the supreme *Nous* or the Mind of the cosmos is like the energizing sun, which sends out its rays without changing its movement. The highest virtue is to renounce the sensible world and to unite the individual soul with the World-Soul through an intensive contemplation. Thus passion or emotion which belongs to the world of sense cannot be a part of the divine. God, who is the perfect Good, is far removed from such feelings as desire and passion.[26] In other words, "pleasure and pain belong neither to the Body nor to the Soul. ... The higher reasonable Soul, in which our personality resides, does not *feel* these sensations, though it is aware of them."[27]

As a result of these investigations, we can conclude that Greek philosophy in general comes to recognize that passion belongs to a lower part of humanity and is, in this sense, unworthy to be claimed by the divine nature. Since passion or feeling has been understood as a bondage of human misery, servitude and imperfection, the concept of divine apathy is eventually accepted by most Greek thinkers in order to defend the goodness of divine nature. Thus, it clearly implies that the idea of impassible God has its root in the notion of divine apathy. As Robinson describes it, "one of these Greek ways was to conceive God as impassible, removed from any capacity to suffer, indeed to feel as men do."[28] It seems, then, reasonable for us to agree with the assertion of Robert Franks that the patripassian movement of the second and third centuries was an attempt to carry through the religious idea of God in opposition to all Greek philosophy.[29]

3. The Static Notion of Divine Autarkeia

The concept of *apatheia* is closely related to the Greek idea of *autarkeia,* which literally means "sufficiency" or "contentment." As we have already stated, the indignity of passion is claimed by the Greek thinkers because of its irrationality and its ability to be affected from outside. The divine has always been thought to be perfect and self-sufficient, so that He cannot be affected or moved by any human desire or emotion. To be affected means for them to be insufficient and discontented. As Aristotle has remarked, "the final good is thought to be self-sufficient" and "the end of action."[30] Thus, God, who represents the

[26] William Ralph Inge, *The Philosophy of Plotinus: The Gifford Lectures at St. Andrews 1917–1918,* Vol. I (London: Longmans, Green and Company, 1929), p. 143.
[27] *Ibid.,* p. 225.
[28] H. Wheeler Robinson, *Suffering, Human and Divine* (New York: The Macmillan Company, 1939), p. 144.
[29] Robert Franks, "Passibility and Impassibility," *Encyclopedia of Religion and Ethics,* Vol. IX, edited by James Hastings (New York: Charles Scribner's Sons, 1924), p. 658.
[30] Aristotle, *op. cit.,* 1097b.

final good, is not only sufficient but immovable. To be self-sufficient means to be in the cessation of movement. In this respect, Aristotelian concept of divine *autarkeia* is based on a static ontology.

We also find a similar notion of divine nature in Plato's thinking. In *The Republic* he discusses whether or not gods appear in various shapes and pass into a number of different forms. In this discourse, he concludes that gods, who are perfect and self-sufficient in every way, cannot change. "Being perfect as he can be, every god, it seems, remains simply and forever in his own form."[31] This changeless and eternal form as the basis of reality has introduced the static notion of divine *autarkeia*. However, the Greek idea of divine *autarkeia* as the absolutely immovable and self-sufficient God was further elaborated by Thomas Aquinas, who defended the doctrine of divine impassibility among the scholastics of the Middle Ages.

Aquinas has not only defended but further clarified the doctrine of divine impassibility on the basis of the perfection and immovability of the divine nature. His concept of immovable God can be traced back to the Aristotelian understanding of God as the "Immovable First Mover."[32] Since God is understood as the "Immovable First Mover," "only God is altogether unchangeable; creatures can all change in some way or other."[33] Things that do change are due to their own potentiality to be realized. In other words, every creature which is changeable has its own potentiality to be perfected. In this sense, God does not have the passive potentiality to be affected or completed. "God is sheer actuality, simply and wholly complete, and not wanting for anything."[34] The divine *autarkeia* simply signifies the nature of this God who is so wholly complete that He wants nothing. On the other hand, *passio* is regarded as a principle for the animal nature of human body which is always accompanied with bodily change. "That is why activities of the sense appetite, because they are bound up with bodily changes, are called passions or emotions."[35] The passions or emotions which involve a constant change are quite contrary to the divine nature which is not only unchangeable but *"purus actus."* To admit the passsibility of God is in reality to make Him imperfect and changeable. Thus Aquinas has defended the traditional doctrine of divine impassibility in terms of the Greek idea of divine *autarkeia*.

Matthews seems to sum up adequately what we have attempted to say when he states that.

---

[31] Plato, *op. cit.*, p. 71.
[32] See Aristotle, *Metaphysics*, Book XI, Chapter 7.
[33] Thomas Aquinas, *Summa Theologica: Latin Text and English Translation, Introductions, Notes, Appendices and Glossaries,* Vol. I (New York: McGraw-Hill Book Company, Inc., 1964), Ia. 9, 3.
[34] *Ibid.,* Ia. 25, 1.
[35] *Ibid.,* Ia. 20, 1.

... the reasons which have led Christian theologians, on the whole, to reject the idea that suffering can enter into the divine experience ... come partly from the tradition, inherited from the Platonic and Aristotelian philosophy, that the essential nature of the divine is to be immutable and self-sufficient.[36]

Besides this Greek idea of the divine nature as the immutable and self-sufficient God, the concept of impassible God can be traced back to Greek anthropology, in which passion is regarded as an inferior element in man. This inferior element cannot be attributed to the divine who is the perfection of the highest good. Thus the concept of *apatheia* is closely interwoven with that of *autarkeia* in the texture of Greek thinking about the divine nature. To sum up, the basic assumptions for the ascription of divine impassibility by the early Church could be said to be mainly the undue emphasis on the distinctions of "persons" in the Trinity, the Greek idea of divine *apatheia* and of divine *autarkeia*.

Some of the Serious Objections Against the Ascription of Divine Passibility

We have dealt with some of the basic issues in the early Christian thought in order to analyze the underlying motives and assumptions for the assertion of the doctrine of divine impassibility. We may now come to consider the question which is somewhat negatively conceived. What are some of the serious objections against the ascription of divine passability? It seems reasonable to conceive that some of these objections are somehow related to the basic assumptions on which the doctrine of divine impassibility is grounded. In this sense, they can be understood as the implications of the assumptions. Thus the question which we seek to answer may help us not only to elaborate the assumptions a little further but to comprehend some of the obstacles to the ascription of a concept of divine passibility. Some of the serious objections may be listed under the three categories as follows: (1) Suffering is an intrinsic evil; therefore, it can not be a part of divine experience. (2) Suffering implies inner frustration; therefore, it cannot be attributed to the divine who is infinite in power and freedom. (3) Suffering implies entanglement in time; therefore, it is incompatible with the God who is totally transcendent. We may consider them separately as briefly as we can.

1. Suffering Is Intrinsically an Evil; Therefore It Cannot Be a Part of Divine Experience

One of the staunch opponents of the concept of divine passibility in the early

---

[36] W. R. Matthews, *God: In Christian Thought and Experiences* (London: Nisbet and Company, 1930), p. 247.

twentieth century was Baron F. von Hügel, whose famous essay on "Suffering and God" had brought a lively debate on the problem of divine passibility. His primary objection against the assertion of divine passibility was in the idea that "suffering is intrinsically an evil."[37] In order to illustrate this idea, he asserted that suffering and sin were similar, because both of them were contrary to the will of God. In this way von Hügel made a strong case against the assertion of divine passibility. His understanding of the divine nature was nothing but perfect Joy and Bliss.

Randles also had made similar statements against the ascription of divine passibility in order to defend the traditional doctrine of divine impassibility. He, like von Hügel, asserted that the nature of suffering itself was basically an evil and was contrary to the very nature of God who was eternal Joy and Delight:

... His enjoyment of His own existence, His delight in action, His pleasure in the good of his creatures, can have no allowing of sorrow, pain, grief or unhappiness. ... Suffering would be a loss of inherent excellence, and is therefore impossible to Him who is absolutely perfect.[38]

From the negative notion of suffering, Randles brought out an interesting issue. He insisted that when we attribute suffering to God, He becomes "the most miserable object of our pity."[39] If God is the most pitiable and greatest sufferer in existence, He cannot be a savior of sufferers. The real issue at stake was the concept of salvation. Therefore, "As against this," Randles said, "our contention is that, while abounding in mercy, as divine He is impassible."[40] Mascall also took a similar view on the problem of divine suffering. Like Randles, Mascall said that, if God ever suffers, either our ultimate destiny would be less than real union with Him or our destiny would be an eternity of suffering with Him.[41]

Thus their objection against the ascription for the conception of divine passibility was due to the idea that suffering was an intrinsic evil, which could not become an instrument of God's saving power.[42] They thought that God,

---

[37] Baron Friedrich von Hügel, "Morals and Religion," *Essays and Addresses on the Philosophy of Religion,* Second Series (London: J. M. Dent and Sons, 1926), p. 199.

[38] Randles, *op. cit.,* pp. 49–50.

[39] *Ibid.,* p. 175.

[40] *Ibid.,* p. 3.

[41] E. L. Mascall, *Existence and Analogy: A Sequel to "He Who Is"* (London: Longmans, Green and Company, 1949), p. 143.

[42] The idea that suffering is an evil is implicit in Greek anthropology, in which emotions or passions take the lower place in human souls. Neither Plato nor Aristotle intended to make passion an evil, but regarded it a lesser good because that which is a less good cannot be a part of God, who is the highest good. Therefore, to make suffering an intrinsic evil is based on the acute form of Greek philosophy.

whose nature is the perfection of good and bliss, could not possess the element of suffering. Thus, God must be impassible.

2. Suffering Implies Inner Frustration; Therefore It Cannot Be Attributed to God, Who Is Infinite in Power and Freedom

One of the most obvious objections against the ascription of a concept of suffering to the divine is to understand suffering as an implication of some kind of frustation that we experience in our life. It is commonly assumed that, if our experience of suffering implies some kind of frustration, the divine experience of suffering may also involve the inner frustration which we experience in suffering. Since frustration implies limitation, God, who is infinite in power and freedom, cannot be frustrated. To attribute frustration to the divine is eventually to limit the power and freedom of God. Limitation also implies weakness. The powerless God is no longer the worthy object of man's dependence. He cannot be the God who is beyond the reach of our failure. Thus we may ask the question that von Hügel has brought to our attention. Shall we not destroy religion if we hold that God Himself is subject to this kind of limitation and frustration?[43] The limitation of power implies also the limitation of freedom, which inevitably accompanies choice. Perfect liberty excludes choice. Choice implies favor, which is quite contrary to the overflowing love of God. Thus to conceive suffering as frustration seems to be one of the most powerful obstacles against the assertion of a concept of divine passibility.[44]

3. Suffering Implies Entanglement in Time; Therefore It Is Incompatible with God Who Is Totally Transcendent

Mozley in the conclusion of his The Impassibility of God has pointed out that one of the motives prompting the assertion of divine impassibility is the belief in the divine transcendence.[45] If God is totally transcendent, He cannot share the sufferings of the world. Thus, Mascall recognizes the difficulty of asserting the suffering of God and of affirming the transcendence of God at the same time. He believes that to attribute suffering to the divine is eventually to deny that God is "genuinely transcendent to, and independent of, the finite world."[46] Robinson also believes that one of the objections against the

---

[43] Von Hügel, op. cit., p. 167 ff.

[44] This objection is a direct implication of the Greek idea of God as autarkeia. The self-sufficient God, whose nature lacks nothing, cannot experience limitation or choice.

[45] Mozley, op. cit., p. 172.

[46] Mascall, op. cit., p. 137.

ascription of divine passibility is that God, who is transcendent, is entangled in the time-process, moving like ourselves.[47] Time and suffering are interwoven with each other. As Whitehead has remarked, "almost all pathos includes a reference to lapse of time."[48] Or in Berdyaev's words, "Time is the child of sin, of sinful slavery, of sinful anxiety."[49] Thus, time is involved in every form of suffering, strife and hardship in the world. If God ever suffers, He must be also entangled in time. Suffering without time is almost unthinkable for us. To believe in divine passibility is, then, to accept that God is in time. For this reason, von Hügel has stressed the significance of divine transcendence. He believes that "Religion itself requires the transcendence of God in a form and a degree which exclude suffering in Him."[50] Consequently, to believe in divine transcendence only is to deny the possibility of divine passibility.

To sum up, some of the serious objections against the ascription of divine passibility are primarily our understanding of suffering as an intrinsic evil, an inner frustration and an entanglement in the time process. They are implicit in the basic assumptions, which become the decisive factors both *for* the assertion of divine impassibility and *against* the concept of divine passibility.

An Examination of the Validity of These Assumptions and Objections in the Light of the Empathy of God

An attempt has been made so far to describe as objectively as possible the basic assumptions for the assertion of divine impassibility and some of the serious objections against the ascription of divine passibility. We may now come to examine the validity of these assumptions and objections in terms of the empathy of God. Since it is not the sympathy but the empathy of God that has become a criterion for the understanding of divine passibility, it seems quite consistent to use also the empathy of God as the criterion to test the validity of these assumptions and objections. Let us begin with the examination of the basic assumptions for the assertion of divine passibility.

1. An Examination of the Validity of the Basic Assumptions for the Assertion of Divine Impassibility in the Light of Divine Empathy

As to the procedure, we may take each of the assumptions separately and consider its validity as briefly and critically as possible. In examining it we

---

[47] Robinson, *op. cit.,* p. 146 ff.
[48] Alfred North Whitehead, *Symbolism, Its Meaning and Effect* (New York: The Macmillan Company, 1927), p. 55.
[49] Nicolas Berdyaev, *The Destiny of Man* (New York: Harper and Brothers, 1960), p. 147.
[50] von Hügel, *op. cit.,* p. 205.

may first restate the assumption as clearly as we can in order to find out basic issues involved in it before we question its validity.

The first assumption which we have defined is the distinction of "persons" in the Trinity. The undue emphasis on the distinction between the Father and the Son by Tertullian and Hippolytus not only helped the early Church to ascribe the doctrine of anti-patripassianism but eventually brought a sharp distinction between the divine and human nature of Jesus Christ. In other words, the christological question was subsequent to the trinitarian distinction, which had first brought a focus to the problem of divine passibility. Thus, the Church had rejected not only the idea that the Father Himself suffered but the idea that the Father suffered with His Son, for they believed that only Christ's manhood had suffered on the Cross. The rejection of the patripassian monarchian idea that the Father Himself suffered on the Cross resulted from the rejection of a modified form of patripassian monarchianism, which asserted the co-suffering of the Father with the Son, prompted an emphasis of the distinction between the divine and human nature in Christ. Therefore, the problem of divine impassibility begins with a specific issue, that is, the distinction of the Son from the Father, but eventually introduces another issue, the distinction of the divine from human nature, which is closely related to the concept of the co-suffering of the Father with the Son. Consequently, we have two specific issues to be considered. The first issue deals with the validity of the sharp distinction of the Father from the Son, and the second has to do with the christological question in relation to the concept of the co-suffering of the Father with the Son.

It is certainly understandable for the early Church to repudiate the heretical advocacy of Modalistic monarchianism by distinguishing clearly between "persons" in the Trinity. Nevertheless, it is quite questionable as to whether or not the Church has distinguished them so sharply as to destroy their mutual participation in their experience of suffering. Nels F. S. Ferré, who has defended the traditional doctrine of divine impassibility, believes that some of modern theology which claims the suffering of God "has failed to distinguish between the Father and the Son."[51] He supports Tertullian's idea that "the Father suffers with the Son is heresy."[52] Does this mean that the mutual participation in and sharing of divine experience between the Son and the Father is destroyed due to the distinction between them? If our answer to this question is "Yes," shall we not then make Christianity a tritheistic rather than a monotheistic religion? The real issue which the early Church has

---

[51] Nels F. S. Ferré, *Evil and the Christian Faith* (New York: Harper and Brothers, 1947), p. 85 ff.
[52] *Ibid.*

presented to us seems to be problem of the tension between a tritheistic and monarchian concept of God. It is certainly questionable whether or not those who defended the doctrine of divine impassibility (or anti-patripassianism) were primarily involved in the polemic against modalistic monarchianism and forgot almost completely that they had also stood in the danger of another kind of heresy, that was, the advocacy of tritheism at the expense of monarchianism. If the error of modalistic monarchians was due to their undue emphasis on the unity of the Father with the Son, then the error of anti-patripassian could be due to their undue emphasis on the distinction of the Son from the Father. These errors are quite easily pointed out by the empathy of God. The empathy of God means neither the merger of one into another to become one, which is the mistake of modalistic monarchians, nor the distinction of one from another to hinder a mutual participation, which is the mistake of anti-patripassians. The archetype of divine empathy signifies the paradoxical unity of experience between the identity and distinction of "persons" in Godhead. It functions as to unite both the Father and the Son without destroying their distinctions, and to distinguish them without destroying their unity. In other words, the "I-Thou" relationship between the Father and the Son in the form of empathy is neither a mutual identification nor a mutual distinction but a mutual involvement through a unity of their experience. The mutual identification destroys their distinctions and the mutual distinction their unity. Nevertheless, the mutual involvement does not destroy any of them but brings them together to co-exist in a paradoxical unity. Therefore, in Johannine sayings, "I and the Father are one" (John 10 : 30) or "He who has seen me has seen the Father" (John 14 : 9) ought to be understood in reference to "I am in the Father and the Father in me" (John 14 : 10−11). As a result, we reject in the light of the empathy of God the validity of both modalistic monarchianism, which asserts the unity without distinctions, and anti-patripassianism, which emphasizes the distinction without a genuine unity.

Let us now consider whether or not a christological question is involved in the first assumption for the assertion of divine impassibility. As we have already indicated, a christological issue was latent, particularly in relation to the "fellow-suffering" of the Father with the Son, even though this fellow-suffering was denied on the basis of the nature of the divine as incapable to suffer.[53] The incapacity of suffering in the Father was affirmed because of His existence as the divine, while the capacity of suffering in the Son was recognized because of His earthly existence *in the flesh*.[54] In other words,

---

[53]   Tertullian, *op. cit.,* Chapter 29.
[54]   *Ibid.*

the humanity of the Son is able to suffer and die, but the divinity, which is the essence of the Father, is unable to suffer and die. Consequently, the denial of the co-suffering of the Father with the Son implies the incapability of Christ's divine nature to experience the suffering of His own human nature. Therefore, our task is to examine the validity of this kind of relationship between the divine and human nature in Jesus Christ in terms of the empathy of God.

If Christ's divine nature is incapable of experiencing the suffering of His humanity, it implies that the former is also unable to share and to participate in the latter. According to the empathy of God, the relationship between the human and divine in Christ is not only mutually inclusive but also mutually participant, in order to unite both of them in the oneness of action and being of Jesus Christ. In other words, in this paradoxical union of experience between the divine and the human in Christ, what the man Jesus experiences is also in the experience of divine nature. It is decisively so, because "God's deity does not exclude, but includes His *humanity*."[55] The suffering of the humanity of Christ must be a part of divine experience, because "his diety *encloses humanity in itself*."[56] Thus we reject in the light of empathy the validity of the idea that the divine nature is unable to share and participate in the suffering of the human nature of Christ. This is why we question the validity of the Chruch's position that the Father as the divine is incapable of sharing the suffering of His Son.

The second assumption for the ascription of divine impassibility is the Greek conception of divine *apatheia*. As we have already said, pathos or feeling has been assigned a lower place in the human soul in Greek philosophy. In contrast to reason, which is regarded as order, light and power to raise man beyond the level of the animal, emotion represents darkness, unruly impulse and disorder, which belong to the animal nature of man. Therefore, according to the Greek idea, feeling or passion is incompatible with the dignity of the divine. It is on this ground that pathos is eliminated from the divine nature. The conception of the absence of passion or pathos in the divine can be, therefore, traced back to the Greek anthropology, in which pathos belongs to the inferior components of humanity. As a result, the motive behind this idea of divine apathy is the dread of anthropomorphism. The fear of anthropomorphism is always associated with the indignity of pathos. Therefore, let us examine, in the light of divine empathy, the validity of the idea that the elimination of pathos or emotion from the divine nature is due to the dread of anthropomorphism.

[55] Karl Barth, *The Humanity of God* (Richmond: John Knox Press, 1960), p. 49.
[56] *Ibid.,* p. 50.

To begin our investigation we may pose the following question: "Is the pathosless divine compatible with the Christian concept of God, who communicates Himself to us in the form of empathy?" As we have said, the God who comes to us in His empathy is no other than *Agape,* which *always* comprises a personal category. Can the God who does not possess feeling or pathos be, then, the God of love? We agree that a feeling is not identical with love, but it is a mode and power of love. The pathos of love is the power of divine participation in the world. In other words, it is the essence of divine empathy, that is, the mode of *Agape* . Thus, "The emotional element cannot be separated from love, love without its emotional quality is 'good will' toward somebody or something, but it is not love."[57] Consequently, God, who does not have an emotion or pathos, is not the God of love. Thus we reject that the Greek concept of divine *apatheia* is compatible with the Christian idea of God who is love.

The rejection of the Greek notion of divine *apatheia* on account of the Christian concept of God as *Agape* raises another question. That is the question about the nature of pathos itself. If pathos represents the irrational and blind impulse, how could we attribute it to the divine who is omniscient? For this question, we first reject the Greek way of thinking about the divine nature. Greek philosophy refuses to attribute pathos to the divine because its reasoning, which is based on the analogy of being, cannot admit such a low quality as pathos to the divine. That is, that the pathos of God is *directly* inferred from human pathos. We have already indicated that this approach, that is, the analogy of being, is contrary to the method of our approach, that is, the analogy of faith. The analogy of faith which we have defined (see Appendix) does not infer directly the divine nature from human attributes, but always conceives it *indirectly* through the manifestation of divine empathy, which is clearly expressed in the being of God-man in Jesus Christ. The pathos of God which we understand from the manifestation of divine empathy, that is, God-man in Christ, is quite different from that which is inferred directly from our experience of human emotions or passions. The pathos of God which we understand from the being of God-man in Christ is not irrational but is "transrational." It is not a blind impulse but a passionate participation to love the unlovable. It does not imply the changing mood of human passion which comes and passes one after another, but it means God's "infinite concern for the time process."[58] The pathos of God is not manifest

---

[57] Paul Tillich, *Systematic Theology,* Vol. III (Chicago: University of Chicago Press, 1963), p. 136.
[58] Emil Brunner, *The Christian Doctrine of God: Dogmatics,* Vol. I, trans. by Olive Wyon (Philadelphia: The Westminster Press, 1950), p. 274.

in sympathy but always in empathy. The sympathy of God implies the identification of divine pathos with human emotion. On the other hand, the
empathy of God signifies not the identification but the participation of
divine pathos in human feeling. It never eliminates the uniqueness of divine
pathos over against the passion or emotion of man. That is why, in the light
of divine empathy, we cannot apply our experience of passion or emotion
directly to the reality of divine pathos. It is not our answer to eliminate pathos
from the divine but to affirm it in spite of our failure to understand it in terms
of our human experience. Therefore, we deny the validity of the concept of
divine *apatheia,* which came from the failure of Greek philosophy to
differentiate divine pathos from human emotion. Moreover, pathos must
be understood as a generic term. It is complete in itself and a total disposition
of oneself. As we have indicated, the feeling that feels or pathos is inclusive
of the cognitive and volitional elements of person.

The last assumption for the ascription of divine impassibility is the static
notion of divine *autarkeia,* which is based on the Greek concept of God.
The static ontological presupposition of divine sufficiency or perfection has
become a controlling factor, especially for Thomas Aquinas, for defending
the doctrine of divine impassibility. The sufficient God does not have any
passive potentiality to be actualized or affected externally. This static notion
of divine perfection as the immovable and unchanging Being is based on the
idea that in God there is no potentiality or receptivity to be affected from
without or actualized within but is *"actus purus."* However, the issue which
has been presented by this assumption is neither the pure action of God nor
the perfection and sufficiency of God but the static ontology which makes
Him to be the immovable and undisturbed Being. Let us, therefore, examine
in the light of divine empathy the validity of the static ontological presupposition of divine perfection as the immovable Being.

The concept of divine empathy is implicit in the idea that God *acts in* the
world. In other words, it presupposes the dynamic ontology, which enables us
to conceive God as the living person who acts in love. Thus, the principle of
divine empathy is based on the concept of God who can move and act
according to His own will. The God whom we understand in Christ is certainly "not like that divinity of platonism who is unconcerned, and therefore
unmoved," but "He alters His behavior in accordance with the changes in
man."[59] Thus "God 'reacts' to the acts of men, and in that He 'reacts,' He
changes."[60] However, the idea of God's reaction to the acts of men ought not
to be understood as being affected by men because of His imperfectness.

[59]   *Ibid.,* p. 268.
[60]   *Ibid.*

God responds to the changing situation of the world, not because in God there is the passive potentiality to be perfected, but because the active potentiality to give Himself in His empathy in spite of men's unwillingness to accept Him. In this respect, men's action never causes or affects but always *occasions* divine "reaction," which is to be understood not as the action against but the action in response to the human action. Divine "reaction" does not represent the weakness or imperfectness of the divine, but rather it signifies the strength and perfection of His personality. It is a sensitiveness of God as a result of His perfect relation to the imperfect creatures. Even though He moves and acts upon human situations, His basic attitude, which is in accordance with His eternal will, is unchangeable. That is why in God there is a paradoxical unity between Being and Becoming, static and dynamic and change and changeless.[61] Therefore, the static notion of divine *autarkeia* is failing to do justice to the dynamic and living God who reveals Himself in Jesus Christ.

2. An Examination of Some of the Serious Objections Against the Assertion of Divine Passibility in the Light of the Empathy of God

Since these objections are implicit in the assumptions, our task here is relative to the examination of the assumptions which we have just undertaken. We may take each of the objections separately as we have done before in order to consider its validity.

The first objection against the assertion of divine passibility is the concept of suffering as an intrinsic evil. If suffering is intrinsically an evil, the God who is the perfection of good cannot suffer since the evil represents the counter force of good. Moreover, those who have attributed to suffering as an intrinsic evil, such as von Hügel and Randles, insist upon the eternal bliss of God over against suffering and misery. For them the eternal bliss represents the intrinsic goodness of God. Thus, the concept of suffering is used as an anti-thesis to that of bliss. As a result, we raise two specific issues to consider in connection with this objection: the first deals with the question of whether suffering is always evil or not, and the second with the relationship between the suffering and bliss of God.

Is suffering always an evil? As we have already made clear in the Introduction of this book, there are generally two categories of suffering: the suffering which is due to evil, and the suffering which is due to a vicarious sacrifice. We have called the former a general suffering and the latter a

---

[61] H. Maurice Relton, *Studies in Christian Doctrine* (London: The Macmillan Company, 1960), p. 22.

redemptive suffering. Both suffering and evil are significantly related to each other. The general suffering (or penal suffering) is *effected* by an evil, while the redemptive suffering is *occasioned* by it. In other words, evil is the cause as well as the condition of suffering. Thus, a general suffering, which is effected by an evil, can be an evil, but the redemptive suffering, which is occasioned by an evil, cannot be an evil. Rather, the latter is intrinsically good, because its purpose is to overcome the evil. This redemptive sacrifice of God is accompanied by the empathy of God, which is fully and perfectly manifest in the coming of God in Jesus Christ. As to the general suffering, we cannot say it is evil or it is not evil. Robinson calls this suffering a "raw material of life," which "will depend entirely on what he himself does with it."[62] Thus, "everything will depend on the attitude of the sufferer and what he does with the raw material given him to shape."[63] The right attitude of a sufferer may produce a positive value, but the wrong attitude may produce the most disastrous evil. Suffering can become an instrument for good to quicken our heart to participate in the empathy of God. At the same time, it may become an instrument of evil to alienate us much farther from God. Consequently, we must reject the idea that suffering in itself is intrinsically an evil.

The other issue which is directly related to this objection is the relationship between the suffering and bliss of God. It has been claimed by some of those who oppose the concept of divine passibility that to attribute suffering to God is contrary to the eternal bliss of God. We intend to examine here whether divine bliss means the absence of suffering in the divine or something else. The concept of divine bliss ought not to be understood in terms of the neoplatonic idea of static ontology. The Christian concept of divine bliss is different from the static notion of peace and tranquillity. In other words, the Christian understanding of divine bliss is not the absence of disturbance in the inner life of God. The living God, whose very nature is to communicate Himself to the world in His empathy, is never happy without being disturbed. The Being of the divine is always active in empathy, because the immovable God is contradictory to the living and personal God in whom we believe. Therefore, divine bliss must be understood in terms of God's active participation in the world. This passionate empathy of God to participate Himself totally in the lives of men in spite of their rebellion is nothing other than the suffering of God, which is an active travail to overcome the evil of the world. This is why divine bliss is not in the exclusion of suffering but inclusion of it to overcome the negative. Tillich is right in saying that a sound approach to this

---

[62]   Robinson, *op. cit.,* p. 182.
[63]   *Ibid.,* p. 195.

question is to "combine the doctrine of eternal blessedness with the negative element without which life is not possible and blessedness ceases to be blessed."[64] The bliss of God is in this eternal conquest and overcoming the evil through His active travail. Thus, "eternal blessedness is not a state of immovable perfection," but it is "through fight and victory."[65] Because the idea of blessedness is implicit in the overcoming through suffering, "suffering does not prevent happiness, but actually, in its own way, contributes to happiness."[66] Thus we conclude that eternal bliss is not the absence of divine suffering but the victory of His suffering over the evil of the world.

The second objection to the ascription of divine passibility is the idea that suffering in our experience implies a frustration. Thus, to ascribe suffering to the divine is also to attribute frustration to Him. If God is infinite in power and wisdom, He cannot be frustrated because a frustration signifies a limitation. Thus, the real issue which is behind this objection is that to believe in divine passibility eventually reduces the infinite to the finite God. Let us, then, examine the validity of this assertion that God's suffering means His frustration on account of His limitation.

Robinson believes that our experience of frustration in suffering cannot be attributed to the divine, because our experience of frustration springs from our physical bodies.[67] Since the divine nature does not have a physical body, He cannot experience frustration as we do. Here, Robinson closely identifies frustration with the concept of pain, which we have already defined in terms of bodily sensations. However, we are not in the position to say that there is not frustration in a non-physical body. If frustration implies a limitation or a lack of something in an entity, we ought not to limit it to a physical body alone. Therefore, we must not hastily reject the idea that there is no element of frustration in the divine, because He is Spirit. We can extend the idea that the limitation or the lack of perfection in the spiritual body also implies a frustration. Again, the basic issue in this objection is the question of divine limitation. However, the real question is not whether God is limited or not, but how He is limited. Is God limited because of a lack of something in His intrinsic nature, or a lack of that which is needed in others? As we have already said, God is self-sufficient and needs nothing for Himself but always gives of Himself for the need of others. Thus, divine toil and suffering do not spring from the limitation of His essential Being but from voluntary self-limitation and self-expression of His love for others. This voluntary limitation

---

[64] Tillich, *Systematic Theology, III*, 404–405.
[65] *Ibid.*, p. 405.
[66] Francis Petit, *The Problem of Evil*, trans. from the French by Christopher Williams (New York: Hawthorn Books, 1958), p. 55.
[67] Robinson, *op. cit.*, p. 148.

of God is a result of His empathy. In other words, the self-limitation of God is subsequent to the empathy of God. *In the empathy of God there is a paradoxical union between the self-sufficiency in His essential nature and the self-limitation in His existential situation.* In this paradox the self-limitation of God cannot be understood as a frustration on account of a lack of His perfection. The suffering of God does not imply the limitation of His essential nature, but it rather signifies His strength to limit Himself in the existential situation. McConnell states it quite simply when he says that if suffering does not reach to God, God is limited.[68] We conclude, therefore, that we should regard divine suffering as not only an inner frustration but an active travail in His empathy. It is not the weakness but the strength of God to love the man who revolts against Him.

The last objection which we have suggested is the idea that suffering implies an entanglement in time-process. Thus, to attribute suffering to the divine means to entangle Him in the process of time. However, if God is wholly transcendent, He cannot be entangled by time. Being in time signifies limitation and change according to the process of time. Thus, those who assert the concept of divine impassibility have denied the possibility of eternal God being in the process of time. However, the real issue which the objection presents to us is the relationship between time and eternity. How can God, who is in eternity, be entangled in time? We may consider this question in the light of divine empathy.

This question can be simply answered by saying that God is in time, because time is in the hand of God. However, this does not mean that time controls God, but God controls Time. In other words, "the reality of God does not in any way depend upon the reality of time," but "the reality of time depends upon the reality of God."[69] It is precisely so, because God's creation includes the creation of time, such as the hours, day and night, summer and winter and the coming ages as in the creation story in Genesis 1. Since God is the Creator of time, He is not a slave of time but becomes voluntarily part of time. Thus, God rules time by participating in time-process.

However, the "God in time" is *always* subsequent to the "time in God." The former represents a temporal time, while the latter an eternal time. In the empathy of God they are not identical but mutually inclusive and participant in each other. In other words, in the empathy of God there is a paradoxical union between the "God in time" and the "time in God." Therefore, "through this indwelling of God," that is, the empathy of God, "eternity

---

[68] Francis J. McConnell, *Is God Limited?* (London: Williams and Norgate, 1924), p. 284.
[69] Bertrand R. Brasnett, *The Suffering of the Impassible God* (London: S. P. C. K., 1928), p. 81.

itself is 'brought within time.'"[70] In other words, the "God in time" is to be conceived as God's voluntary and self-giving travail to bring time in His eternity. Therefore, God can be both in time and in eternity.

As a result of our critical investigation of the validity of the assumptions for the assertion of divine impassibility and the objections to the ascription of divine passibility, we come to agree with Donald Baillie's general remark on the problem of divine passibility. He has stated in his *God Was in Christ* that "I cannot but think (in spite of Baron von Hügel's impressive protest) that there is some truth in the wide spread modern tendency to modify the impassibility doctrine."[71] The failure of the doctrine of divine impassibility can be traced back to the basic mode of theological thinking, which has its root in the category of platonic philosophy. Out of the rational and static ontology of Greek philosophy the doctrine of divine impassibility was formulated in the early Church. Therefore, Relton is quite right when he says, "The abstract concept of the impassibility of God is based on a metaphysical idea, while the passibility of personal God is evidenced in the biblical idea."[72] If we believe that the New Testament witness to revelation is the basis and the content of all dogmatics, the problem of divine passibility ought to be an expression of the biblical witness and not a speculation of platonic philosophy. The empathy of God, which is the category of biblical witness, is quite contrary to the category of platonic philosophy. The empathy of God is based on a faithfilled, personal and dynamic ontology, while platonic philosophy is based on a rational, impersonal and static ontology. Therefore, we conclude with Fairbairn's statement that "Theology has no falser idea than that of the impassibility of God. ... The very truth that came by Jesus Christ may be said to be summed up in the passibility of God."[73]

[70] Emil Brunner, *The Christian Doctrine of the Church, Faith, and the Consummation: Dogmatics,* Vol. III, trans. by David Cairns (Philadelphia: The Westminster Press, 1960), p. 378.
[71] Donald M. Baillie, *God Was in Christ* (New York: Charles Scribner's Sons, 1948), pp. 198–199.
[72] Relton, *op. cit.,* p. 180.
[73] A. M. Fairbairn, *The Place of Christ in Modern Theology* (New York: Charles Scribner's Sons, 1893), p. 483.

CHAPTER III

THE AFFIRMATION OF DIVINE PASSIBILITY: ITS COMPATIBILITY WITH THE MAJOR DOCTRINES OF THE CHRISTIAN FAITH

As a result of our critical examination of the validity of the basic assumptions for the doctrine of divine impassibility and some of the serious objections against the assertion of divine passibility in the light of divine empathy, we have concluded that the traditional idea of divine impassibility is largely based on a metaphysical notion of deity rather than the biblical idea of God. Therefore, we have rejected the impassibility of God as a sound doctrine of the Christian faith.

Our task here is to see whether or not the concept of divine passibility is *compatible* with the major doctrines of the Christian faith, namely the doctrines of creation, incarnation, atonement, the Holy Spirit and the Trinity. However, it is intented neither to postulate the concept of divine passibility from these doctrines nor to produce a new view of these doctrines, but to see the relationship between them in the light of the empathy of God. If the concept of divine passibility is the biblical idea of God, it must be in conformity with those doctrines of the Christian faith. Thus, to test the compatibility of divine passibility with major doctrines of the Christian faith is, in a way, to see the validity of the concept of divine passibility in terms of a comprehensive perspective. In order to do this, we may first examine the relationship between the empathy of God and these doctrines. Secondly, a sound argument against the doctrine of divine impassibility is to be presented in terms of this relationship. Finally, the compatibility of the concept of divine passibility with the essential meanings of these doctrines is to be examined in the light of the empathy of God. We may take each of these doctrines separately and examine it as briefly as possible.

Creation and Divine Passibility

Let us first examine the relationship between the biblical meaning of creation and the concept of divine empathy as we have defined it.

1. Creation as the External Manifestation of Divine Empathy

We cannot deny that creation is an event, not in time but with time, for time is also God's creation. Creation is certainly the event which has taken place in eternity. But the essential meaning of the story of creation in Genesis is not the event but the relationship between the Creator and creatures. In this respect, Paul Tillich is quite right to say that "The doctrine of creation is not the story of an event which took place 'once upon a time.' It is the basic description of the relationship between God and the world"[1] This relationship between the Creator and creatures, that is, the essential meaning of the biblical story of creation, presupposes the empathic relationship of God. This empathic relationship of God to be for us means the transition of God's being "as-He-is-in-Himself" to His "being-for-us."[2] The first effect of this transition is the essential meaning of creation.[3] In other words, creation means the actualization of God's gracious will to impart Himself for us. His will to be for us, which is essentially rooted in His very nature to give Himself for others, is materially manifest in the empathy of God as the creation of God. Therefore, creation means the first and external manifestation of the empathic self-communication of God to participate and communion with us, whose very existence is determined by His will to be for us. Creation is, then, an external re-enactment of the primordial empathic relationship which has existed in Godhead in eternity.

Furthermore, this empathic self-communication of God is realized in the covenant, which represents an internal and formal expression of creation. "The heart of the biblical idea of the covenant," as Brunner has clearly pointed out, is "the realization of the divine self-communication and sovereignty in communion with and amongst men."[4] Thus, the covenant is more than a mere form of agreement between the Creator and creatures through the law. It essentially means the formal realization of divine empathy, which creates the community of divine-human participation. In other words, the internal manifestation of divine empathy, which is the essential meaning of covenant, creates "a genuine community, in which the voice of the partner, the human 'Thou,' is also heard."[5] This genuine community of divine participation in which we are called to participate as His partners is an internal basis of

---

[1] Tillich, *Systematic Theology, I,* 252.
[2] Brunner, *Dogmatics, II,* 4.
[3] Emil Brunner defines the creation as the first effect of God's being for us from His being-in-Himself. "The first effect of this being God 'for us' is the creation." See Brunner, *Dogmatics, I,* 193.
[4] Brunner, *Dogmatics, II,* 216.
[5] *Ibid.*

creation. Therefore, if the creation is the external basis of the covenant, the covenant is the internal basis of creation.[6] Both creation and covenant mutually complement each other in order to express fully the first effect of divine empathy, which has existed in Godhead before the beginning of the world. The creation is the external and material manifestation of divine empathy, while the covenant is the internal expression of divine empathy.

2. *The Incompatibility of the Concept of Divine Impassibility with the Doctrine of Creation and Providence*

We have briefly stated the fundamental relationship between the doctrine of creation and the concept of divine empathy. We may now try to apply this relationship to examine whether or not the doctrine of divine impassibility is compatible with the essential meaning of creation as we have defined. Since the doctrine of creation is intimately related with that of providence, we may also examine whether the doctrine of providence is or is not in accordance with the concept of divine impassibility.

The essential meaning of creation in the Scripture is understood in terms of the empathic relationship between the Creator and creatures. Since we understand the creation as the first effect or manifestation of God's empathic self-communication to be with us and for us, it is contrary to assume that the creation implies the gulf which separates the Creator from creatures. Rather, the creation signifies the effect of the empathic community in which we are called to participate in His participation. Thus, the impassible God, who is often identified with the immovable and absolute Deity who is indifferent to His creature, is quite contrary to the biblical understanding of God as the Creator. Since creation means the effect of His coming to be for us, "God does not stand outside the range of human suffering and sorrow. He is personally involved in, even stirred by, the conduct and fate of man."[7] If God participates in His creatures, He is the One who is concerned with everything, because He lives in and with them. In the perfect empathy of God, as Weatherhead said, "the sufferings of men are the sufferings of God."[8] Thus we conclude that the God of creation as witnessed in the Scripture is neither the exalted impassible God who is separated from the world by an unbridgeable gulf, nor the impersonal Absolute who cannot be touched by the sufferings of the world, but He is the loving God who participates in and shares with the infirmities of the world which He has created.

---

[6]   Barth, *Church Dogmatics, III/I,* 42ff, 94ff, 228ff.
[7]   Abraham J. Heschel, *The Prophets* (New York: Harper and Row, 19627, p. 224.
[8]   Leslie D. Weatherhead, *Why Do Men Suffer?* (New York: The Abingdon Press, 1936), p. 127.

If the doctrine of creation means the original effect of the empathic communication of God to be with us and for us, the doctrine of providence means God's affirmation of that effect. In other words, creation presupposes providence, and providence is subsequent to creation. Thus, they are inseparably related to each other. The essential meaning of providence is the constant affirmation of divine empathy through a permanent activity of God in creation. The affirmation of the empathic relationship of God to the world is, so to speak, "the original gospel," that is, "God cares!"[9] God cares and passionately involves Himself in the affairs of the world, because He affirms the goodness of His creation. This is why He cannot refuse to bear the sufferings of His own creatures, for His refusal to do so is in a way to deny the goodness of His creatures. Certainly, a creator God who refused to bear suffering for the goodness of His creatures would be less than good.[10] Consequently, the doctrine of providence essentially means, "God does not stand outside the world serenely contemplating the misery and strife."[11] That is, in other words, "He does not leave this world to suffer while He remain at ease apart,"[12] but all the suffering and joy of the world is within the experience of God. Thus, the essential meaning of divine providence radically denounces any assertion of the impassible God whose act is not a fatherly care but absolute determinism. As a result, we conclude that the traditional doctrine of divine impassibility is incompatible with the biblical understanding of both creation and providence.

3. Evil as the Providential Occasioning of Divine Passibility

Since the problem of evil is directly related not only with the doctrine of creation and providence but with the concept of divine passibility, we intend to examine how the problem of divine passibility is related to the reality of evil in the world. The task at which we aim is, therefore, neither the problem of theodicy, which means the defense of divine justice and righteousness in face of the reality of evil in the world, nor the question of whether suffering is good or evil, which we have already discussed in the previous chapter, but the relationship between evil and divine passibility. This relationship is to be understood not in terms of mutual inclusiveness but in terms of irrevocable order. In other words, the passibility of God is always subsequent to the reality of evil, while the reality of evil does not always presuppose the passibil-

---

[9]   Robert C. Dentan, *The King and His Cross* (New York: Seabury Press, 1965), p. 44.
[10]   Bertrand R. Brasnett, *The Suffering of the Impassible God* (London: S. P. C. K., 1928), p. 92.
[11]   J. K. Mozley, *The Impassibility of God: A Survey of Christian Thought* (Cambridge: University Press, 1926), p. 161.
[12]   *Ibid.,* p. 154.

ity of God. The possibility of God is always a result of His voluntary and providential care, because evil does not have power to cause suffering to God but only to occasion it. This is why we would like to think of evil as the providential occasioning of divine passibility.

The word "evil" is generally used in opposition to good. In other words, what is not good is commonly understood as evil. If we understand goodness as the fulfillment of our own *telos*, that is, the actualization of our own potentialities, we can conceive evil as something quite contrary to this. The biblical notion of evil is also the antithesis of good, as it has been introduced in the symbol of the tree of the knowledge of good and evil in Genesis 2 : 17. Evil can be divided into two kinds: natural evil and moral evil. The natural evil corresponds to worthlessness and corruption (II Kings 2 : 19; Proverbs 20 : 14; Jeremiah 24 : 2; Matthew 6 : 23, and others), harmfulness, trouble and distress (Genesis 26 : 29; 31 : 7; Deuteronomy 26 : 6; I Samuel 18 : 10, and others), which result from the destructive force of nature. On the other hand, moral evil, which is a theological name for sin, has to do with our relation to others, especially to God (Genesis 19 : 7, 44 : 5; Deuteronomy 26 : 6; Judges 11 : 27, and others). The source of evil is often the devil or satan, who re-presents the personification of evil.[13] The New Testament expression of the demonic power which Christ has struggled to overcome cannot be completely eliminated as a myth. Whatever it may be understood in our day as the "collective unconsciousness"[14] or the "distortion in the structure of existence,"[15] we cannot deny the existential reality of evil force in the world. Thus, we acknowledge that there is the force which constantly opposes the will of God. Evil is, as Brunner said, "the product of apostasy from God, of the perversion of the divine order of creation."[16] Whether the origin of evil comes from the "misused gift of human freedom,"[17] from "nonbeing entered the created world,"[18] from the activity of "the Given,"[19] or from the "transi-

---

[13] The Greek word "δαιμόνιον" is commonly used in the Gospels (Matthew 11 : 18; Luke 7 : 33; 8 : 27, and others), while the use of both "ἀρχαί" and "ἐξουσίαι" appears in Pauline thought (Romans 8 : 38; Ephesians 3 : 10, 6 : 12; Colossians 1 : 16, 2 : 15, and others). Besides these demonic beings and cosmic powers, there is the supreme demonic being, which the Johannine writer describes as "ὁ ἄρχων τοῦ κόσμου τούτου" (John 12 : 31, 14 : 30, 16 : 11). The synoptists call it " ὁ ἄρχων τῶν δαιμονίων " (Matthew 9 : 34, 12 : 24; Mark 3 : 22; Luke 11 : 15, and others), who is designated as " βεεζεβούλ ." This satan is identical with "the adversary" (Job 1–2; Zechariah 3 : 1), who is the chief source of evil. See Jung Young Lee, "Interpreting the Demonic Powers in Pauline Thought," in *Novum Testamentum,* Vol. XII, Fasc. 1 (January, 1970), pp. 54–69.

[14] Brunner, *Dogmatics, II,* 142–143.

[15] Allan D. Galloway, *The Cosmis Christ* (New York: Harper and Brothers, 1951), p. 29.

[16] Brunner, *Dogmatics, II,* 181.

[17] *Ibid.*

[18] Nicolas Berdyaev, *The Destiny of Man* (New York: Harper and Brothers, 1960), pp. 29–30.

[19] Edgar S. Brightman, *A Philosophy of Religion* (Englewood Cliffs, New Jersey: Prentice-Hall, Inc., 1940), p. 336 ff.

tion from essence to existence,"[20] the essential meaning of evil is the negative and self-destructive force which "God Himself opposes and contradicts its onslaught on His creation."[21] Thus it is the object of God's eternal "No." Yet, this "No" is inseparable from God's eternal "Yes." This is, then, the paradoxical unity which transcends human cognition.

If we believe that the meaning of evil is the negation of divine goodness, and the existential reality of evil is the actual experience of men, we cannot avoid concluding that God in His empathy is engaged in the struggle with us to overcome it. This struggle of God to preserve the goodness of His creation over against the destructive force of evil is to be understood as His vicarious suffering through His providential care. In other words, divine passibility is providentially occasioned by the assertion of the evil force to destroy the goodness of His creation. As long as there is evil in the world, God suffers because of His nature to participate in the world. Relton seems to connect both divine suffering and human sin too closely. "He is suffering now. Why? Because we *continue* to sin. He will cease to suffer if and when we cease to sin. If we repent He will smile!"[22] The similar view is also expressed by Robinson, who says that "the actuality we call sin is existent within God only as suffering."[23] The danger of such an intimate connection between human sin and divine suffering is to reduce them in terms of a cause and effect relationship. However, the suffering of God is not caused or controlled by the power of human sins. In other words, "this divine suffering is not caused but evoked by a lack of congruity between God and the condition of the world and man."[24] What we intend to stress here is that evil, whether it is the human or natural evil, does not have power to cause but to *occasion* God to suffer, for it is God's own nature to fight against the power of evil. Even though divine suffering is not caused by evil, it is "the God who Himself suffers pain because of our sin and guilt."[25] Without evil there is no suffering in the divine. Therefore, if we believe in the reality of evil which opposes the order of creation, we cannot escape the idea that the God who wills to participate Himself in the world to preserve the goodness of creation eventually suffers with us. His suffering is occasioned by the reality of evil which is paradoxically united with the reality of good. God's suffering, then, begins

---

[20] Tillich, *Systematic Theology, II*, 29.
[21] Barth, *Church Dogmatics, IV/2*, 225.
[22] H. Maurice Relton, *Studies in Christian Doctrine* (London: The Macmillan Company, 1960), pp. 82–83.
[23] H. Wheeler Robinson, *Suffering, Human and Divine* (New York: The Macmillan Company, 1939), p. 178.
[24] Nicolas Berdyaev, *The Divine and Human* (London: Geoffrey Bless, 1949), p. 73.
[25] Barth, *Church Dogmatics, II/I*, 373.

with the order of creation, the goodness, which presupposes the evil, the chaos of the world.

Incarnation and Divine Passibility

The incarnation of God in Christ is the very essence of our Christian faith and the final form of divine revelation. It is, in this respect, very significant to examine the relationship between the doctrine of incarnation and the concept of divine passibility in the light of the empathy of God.

1. Incarnation as the Perfect Analogy of the Empathy of God

Anyone who takes the doctrine of incarnation seriously does not deny that the incarnation of God has taken place in a specific time and place as the most miraculous event in history. Its significance as an historical event, which has separated the old from the new perspective of life, cannot be readily dismissed. However, the essential meaning of incarnation is not the event itself but the event with the new relationship between God and man. The event of incarnation discloses that new relationship which God Himself initiates by coming Himself to become a man in Jesus Christ. Thus, the real meaning of incarnation is not to be understood as the miraculous event of Christmas once upon a time, but as the faithful and unbroken relationship between God and man through the complete and perfect participation of the divine pathos in human experience. In this respect, the meaning of incarnation is nothing else than the most perfect form of divine empathy, the unity of experience between man and God, which is perceived by us only through the analogy of faith. Incarnation means, then, the genuine and perfect analogy of divine empathy.

   In order to illustrate the meaning of incarnation as the perfect analogy of divine empathy, let us take two prominent passages on the concept of incarnation in the New Testament: Paul's epistle to the Philippians (2 : 6–8) and the prologue of John (1 : 1–18). In both passages we may get a false impression that incarnation means simply God's becoming man. If incarnation means "God has become man," as Tillich eloquently pointed out, it is "not a paradox of the Christian message but a non-sensical statement."[26] The real meaning of incarnation as witnessed in these passage of the New Testament ought not to be understood as the transformation of divine into human but as the participation of the divine in the "flesh" or in the "form of servant." It is not

[26]   Tillich, *Systematic Theology, II*, 94.

the transformation but the perfect participation of divine pathos in human existence to form a unity. Barth is certainly right. "There is nothing said about an intermixing of God and man, or a changing of God into a man, or of a man into God, but simply this — that without ceasing to be God, God becomes and is at the same time man."[27] The Johannine statement that "the Word became flesh" (John 1 : 14) does not mean the "Logos" changes into man. The statement must be understood in relation to the following statement that the Word "dwelt among us," which signifies the participation of the Word in us rather than the transformation of it. Therefore, the essential meaning of the word "became" in John 1 : 14 is to be understood as *"be-came,"* which implies the coming of God into human existence in the perfect form of empathy. Tillich is correct in saying that the word "'became' points to the paradox of God participating in that which did not receive him and in that which is estranged from him."[28] The significance of incarnation is associated with the word "come." "The fact that 'God comes' is one of the fundamental facts of the Biblical Revelation."[29] Jesus spoke His own coming: "I am come" to call sinners (Matthew 9 : 13), or "the son of man came" to serve rather than to be served (Matthew 20 : 28). In incarnation the coming of God is manifest in terms of empathy. That is the *coming* of God into man to *be* "the likeness of sinful flesh" (Romans 8 : 3). In other words, the paradox of incarnation is the coming of the divine into human history to be a man without ceasing to be God at the same time. As Pannenberg attempts to say, the union between God and man in Jesus is indirect or dialectic in nature.[30] This coming is not the ascent of man to God but the descent of God to man.[31] God descends Himself totally to be in us. Thus, in incarnation the perfect form of divine self-participation is fully realized in history. This historical realization of divine self-participation is to be understood as the perfect empathy of God. Because incarnation is the most perfect symbol of divine empathy, all the empathic relationship between God and man is dependent on it. In other words, it is the key to God's coming in man as well as man's being in God. The meaning of incarnation as the perfect analogy of divine empathy is well illustrated in the Pauline statement: "in him the whole fulness of deity dwells bodily, and you have come to fulness of life in him" (Colossians 2 : 9, 10). Or, in Brasnett's own words, "instead of remaining in cold isolation, complete in his own self-sufficiency, God enters into a warm, close, personal

[27] Karl Barth, *Credo* (New York: Charles Scribner's Sons, 1962), p. 66.
[28] Tillich, *Systematic Theology, II,* 95.
[29] Brunner, *Dogmatics, II,* 351.
[30] Wolfhart Pannenberg, *Jesus — God and Man,* trans. by L. L. Wilkins and D. A. Priebe (Philadelphia: The Westminster Press, 1968), p. 334 ff.
[31] Barth, *Credo,* p. 66.

connection with man by becoming as man."[32] This is precisely what the Johannine statement, "the word became flesh and dwelt among us," may mean to us.

2. *The Incompatibility of the Concept of Divine Impassibility with the Doctrine of Incarnation*

We have stated that the essential meaning of incarnation is not the transformation of God into man but the historical actualization of divine self-participation in human existence. Therefore, we have defined it as the most perfect analogy of divine empathy. Let us now examine the relationship of this perfect analogy with the idea of divine impassibility.

If incarnation means the perfection of divine self-participation in human existence, the gap between the finite and infinite must be overcome. In this unity God and man are no longer co-existing side by side but true God is also a true man.[33] In other words, what the true God in Christ *wills, thinks* and *feels* is also what the true man in Christ *wills, thinks* and *feels*. "Whatever Jesus was or did, in His life, in His teaching, in His Cross and passion, in His resurrection and ascension and exaltation, it is really God that did it in Jesus; that is how the New Testament speaks."[34] In incarnation both divine and human are not only united in will and thought but in pathos.

How can we then say that the suffering of Christ did not touch His deity? Is not the experience of His humanity that of His divinity, if they are genuinely united in perfect empathy? If in incarnation "God's deity does not exclude, but includes His humanity,"[35] how can we say that the suffering of His humanity is not included in His deity? To deny the unity of experience between human and divine in Christ is in a way to deny the reality of incarnation. It is the most dangerous heresy to tear the elements of divine and human apart, for an incarnation is the essence of our Christian faith. Certainly, such a misinterpretation of the divine-human relationship in Jesus Christ is untenable and derogatory to the honor of God, who appeared to suffer but in reality enjoyed a blessed peace.[36] If God was really in Christ to reconcile the world to Himself (II Corinthians 5 : 19), the experience of God could be also in the suffering of Christ. Thus, Mozley is right: "if God had been so wholly present in Jesus Christ that, during the incarnation, God was Jesus and was not to be

---

[32] Brasnett, *op. cit.*, pp. 27–28.
[33] Barth, *Church Dogmatics, 1/2*, 150.
[34] Donald M. Baillie, *God Was in Christ* (New York: Charles Scribner's Sons, 1948), p. 67.
[35] Karl Barth, *The Humanity of God* (Richmond: John Knox Press, 1960), p. 49.
[36] Bertrand R. Brasnett, *The Suffering of the Impassible God* (London: S. P. C. K., 1928), pp. 35–36.

found anywhere else, the belief in a divine, impassible nature could not longer be retained."[37]

If the essence of God is *Agape,* the incarnation is nothing else than the incarnation of *Agape.* Therefore, "it is important to emphasize that for faith the incarnation means the incarnation of divine love."[38] It was the love of God which stooped down to take the form of a servant. The act of this condescending love to be in the lowliest human condition is to be understood as the perfection of divine empathy. This love must then participate in the infirmities of sinful flesh and share human sufferings as its own. "In forgiving us, he takes our sins unto himself. . . . This is the suffering of God."[39] "In this sense the revelation of God in Christ was forever a refutation of His impassibility, since it was a revelation of Love Himself Incarnate."[40] Certainly, the deeper understanding of the incarnation with its revelation of *Agape* as the unity of Christ with the Father would make the doctrine of divine impassibility almost impossible. Therefore, the doctrine of divine impassibility is incompatible with the concept of incarnation as the perfect analogy of divine empathy.

We conclude our examination with the statement of Brasnett, who seems to summarize our points of view.

For ourselves we frankly abandon that difficult conception of the early Church that Christ was passible in His human nature and impassible in His divine. We abandon it because we believe it to be out of harmony with the evidence, to introduce an intolerable dualism in the person of Christ, and to rob the incarnation of most of its religious and moral value.[41]

3. Incarnation as the Historical Basis of Divine Passibility

The meaning of incarnation as the perfect realization of divine self-participation in history repudiates any idea that the empathic relationship of God with the world begins with the incarnation of God in Christ. God's empathic relationship with the world begins with His creation of the world. Since the passibility of God is subsequent to the empathy of God, the incarnation of God in Christ, which symbolizes the second effect of God's empathic re-

---

[37] Mozley, *op. cit.,* p.29.
[38] Gustaf Aulén, *The Faith of the Christian Church,* trans. by Eric H. Wahlstrom and G. Everett Arden (Philadelphia: The Muhlenberg Press, 1948), p. 212.
[39] Bernard M. Loomer, "Christian Faith and Process Philosophy," in *Process Philosophy and Christian Thought,* edited bu Delwin Brown, *et al.* (New York: The Bobbs-Merrill, 1971), p. 87.
[40] H. Maurice Relton, *A Study in Christology: The Problem of the Relation of the Two Natures in the Person of Christ* (New York: The Macmillan Company, 1931), p. 57.
[41] Brasnett, *op. cit.,* p. 34.

lationship with the world, is not the embarkation of divine passibility but the historical actualization of it. Therefore, incarnation is the historical basis of divine passibility.

If we believe that "the incarnation was thus the result of a movement of divine compassion in the very heart of God,"[42] the love of the Father had certainly suffered for evil even prior to the coming of the Son to the world. The Johannine statement that "God so loved the world that he gave his only Son" (John 3 : 16) seems to imply that the long suffering of the Father's love for the world did not begin with the sending of His Son, but the sending of the Son was a result of His suffering love. In other words, divine passibility was not the consequence of incarnation but the incarnation was the consequence of divine passibility. "For if he had not suffered he would not have entered into full participation in human life. He first suffered, then, he came down and was manifested."[43] The incarnation is certainly not the beginning of divine passibility but the continuation of it with an intensification in time and space. Brunner is right to say that the passibility of God is the historical attribute of God's faithfulness to the world. That is in Brunner's own words, "the long-suffering of God is nothing less than the *possibility of history.*"[44] History is the beginning of divine passibility, but the incarnation is the continuation of it in the actual experience of man Jesus Christ. In incarnation the divine experience of suffering for the sins of the world enters into the experience of man. However, it is not the transference but the empathic participation of divine suffering in man Jesus Christ. In other words, in the incarnation the suffering of His divinity, which is in unity with the suffering of His Father, comes to participate in His humanity in such a perfect manner that the suffering of His divinity is also the suffering of His humanity at the same time. This is certainly the paradoxical union of the divine and human suffering in the coming of God in Christ. This paradox repudiates any attempt to separate the suffering of Jesus' humanity from that of His divinity. It also safeguards against the assertion that the incarnation is only the beginning of divine passibility.[45] The "Word" which became flesh

---

[42] H. Maurice Relton, *Studies in Christian Doctrine* (London: The Macmillan Company, 1960), p. 86.

[43] Origen, "Homilies in Ezechielem," *The Early Christian Fathers: A Selection from the Writings of the Fathers from St. Clement of Rome to St. Athanasius,* edited by Henry Bettenson (London, Oxford University Press, 1956), p. 256.

[44] Brunner, *Dogmatics, I,* 274.

[45] For example, James Hinton seems to imply that the suffering of God was manifested at His incarnation. "He emptied Himself, and the pain became manifested; He put off His perfection, and the sorrow was hidden and lost in the fullness of His life no more." See his *The Mystery of Pain* (Boston: Cupples, Upham, and Company, 1886), p. 51. Here "pain" implies our understanding of "suffering."

and dwelt among us (John 1 : 14) was not the word of a pious deity, but it was, as Barth said, "the Word of the Suffering Witness to the truth."[46] It was the Word of the suffering God, which had entered in Christ to embrace every human suffering in the world. As Knight said, in the incarnation "all the striving, toiling and suffering of humanity enters into the heart of the divine experience."[47] Thus, in incarnation the divine experience of suffering is realized in the heart of man, so that the suffering of humanity may enter in the heart of divine experience. If the Word which was manifest in the flesh was the Word of the suffering God, the doctrine of incarnation without the concept of divine suffering, which was latent in the Word, might become an empty formula. However, the reality of the miraculous Christmas is the coming of the suffering God who was born in the very place which men usually abhor, that is, the birth of Christ in a manger because there was no room for him in the inn (Luke 2 : 7).

Atonement and Divine Passibility

The word "atonement," which is not used in the New Testament (R.S.V.) at all, is used here to designate the theological meaning of a reconciliation after a period of estrangement. The concept of atonement as the reconciliation or the restoration of the right relationship between God and man in Christ has been one of the most difficult doctrines to define in the Church. "This is why the Church instinctively refused to state the doctrine of atonement in definite dogmatic terms, as in the case of the Christological dogma."[48] Our task here, however, is neither a clarification of the issues in the doctrine nor a further explication of the nature of this doctrine, but the relationship of the doctrine with the concept of divine passibility. In other words, we basically seek to examine the relationship of the essential meaning of atonement with that of divine passibility. Since the Cross is the central symbol of atonement, we may begin our examination with the meaning of the Cross. We may, then, see whether the concept of divine impassibility is compatible or incompatible with it. Finally, we may study carefully the relationship of the doctrine of atonement with the concept of divine passibility.

1. The Cross as the Depth of Divine Empathy

The Cross is, as Brunner said, "the shortest summary of the whole life of

---

[46] Barth, *Church Dogmatics, IV/3,* 391.
[47] Harold Knight, *The Hebrew Prophetic Consciousness* (London: Lutterworth Press, 1947), p. 147.
[48] Tillich, *Systematic Theology, II,* 170.

Jesus."[49] It is not only one of the indespensable elements in salvation but the climax of divine revelation in history. It represents both the highest revelation of divine love for our recemption and the deepest penetration of divine empathy into our sins. In other words, "The meaning of the Cross is first of all the revelation of the incomprehensible, unconditional love of God."[50] And, at the same time, this incomprehensible love of God unconditionally seeks to participate in men who are utterly alienated from Him. This love of God which is revealed in the Cross is not love in general but the *"Agape* of the Cross,"* that is, the depth of divine empathy. Since the *Agape* of the Cross represents the highest expression of *Agape,* it also implies the deepest dimension of divine self-participation in the world. In this respect, the Cross or "the *Agape* of the Cross" is neither the love of God alone nor the divine passibility alone, but the synthesis of both. The synthesis of the love and the suffering of God is well illustrated in Romans 5 : 6−10:

While we were yet helpless, at the right time Christ died for the ungodly. Why, one will hardly die for a righteous man—though perhaps for a good man one will dare even to die. But God shows his love for us in that while we were yet sinners Christ died for us. Since, therefore, we are now justified by his blood, much more shall we be saved by him from the wrath of God. For if while we were enemies we were reconciled to God by the death of his Son, much more, now that we are reconciled, shall we be saved by his life.

In this passage divine love and divine passibility are united in the death of Christ on the Cross. Therefore, if we ask what *Agape* is, we point to divine passibility on the Cross. And, if we ask what divine passibility is, we point to *Agape* on the Cross. In the Cross of Christ they do not conflict but mutually include each other. In other words, the meaning of the Cross as the depth of divine empathy implies paradoxically the unconditional penetration of divine love into the ultimate negativities of human existence. The death of God-man in Christ on the Cross symbolizes one of the greatest paradoxes of our Christian faith. In the depth of divine empathy we die with His death to sin and live with His resurrection to God (Romans 6 : 10).

   The Cross as the depth of divine empathy denies any assertion that the Cross is the event which has happened once upon a time in history. It means more than the mere event on Calvary. It is the eternal Cross in the heart of God. By the eternal cross we mean "not just the one supreme event on Calvary but the Cross which Jesus carried in his heart from the beginning."[51] The eternal Cross is, what Dinsmore calls, "a Cross in the heart of God

---

[49]   Brunner, *Dogmatics, II,*   282.
[50]   *Ibid.,* p. 295.
[51]   Francis J. McConnel, *Is God Limited?* (London: Williams and Norgate, 1924), p. 289.

before there was one planted on the green hill outside Jerusalem."[52] Since it is elected because of evil, it will remain so long as there is evil in the world. In the eternal love of God there is a lamb slain from the foundation of the world (Revelation 13 : 8) and this lamb slaying will continue because of the continual aggressiveness, intolerance and cruelty of man. This eternal Cross, which represents the depth of divine empathy, is the inner act of God. This inner reality was externalized on the hill of Calvary. In other words, the eternal Cross is the prototype of the historic Cross, which is "the reflection of an act within Godhead."[53] The Cross of Calvary *always* points to the eternal Cross. Thus, Kitamori writes, "The Cross is in no sense an external act of God, but an act within Himself."[54] The reality of the Cross is not the external event of Golgatha but the eternal Cross, which is a center of God's eternal love for the world. If the existential notion of divine suffering points to the historical Cross on the hills of Calvary, the essential meaning of divine suffering points to the eternal Cross, which represents the inner experience of divine love to participate in the bottom of our existential estrangement.

2. The Incompatibility of the Concept of Divine Impassibility with the Reality of the Cross

As we have said, the essential meaning of the Cross points to the inner experience of God to participate in the sinful existence of man at all costs. This inner travail of God represents the eternal Cross, that is, the prototype of the Cross, standing behind the historical event of salvation. The redemptive suffering of Christ on the Cross is a temporal manifestation of the eternal Cross, which is first elected in God because of evil in the world. "We see that Calvary is but the concrete expression in time and space of a great reality, i.e., that God suffers because of man's sin."[55] The suffering and death of Christ on the Cross point to the eternal reality, that is, the eternal suffering and death of God on the eternal Cross. It is certainly astonishing news that God has suffered and died on the Cross. As Kitamori said, "It is impossible for us to understand the logic of Paul completely unless the death of Christ means the death of God Himself."[56] If the reality of the Cross points to the suffering as well as the death of God Himself, how can we justify the idea that God is dead on the Cross? As the Cross of Christ is the reflection of the eternal Cross of God, the suffering and death of Christ are also experienced in the inner

---

[52] Donald M. Baillie, *op. cit.,* p. 194; quoted originally from Charles Allen Dinsmore, *Atonement in Literature and Life,* p. 232.

[53] P. T. Forsyth, *The Person and Place of Jesus Christ* (London: Independent Press, 1909), p. 270.

[54] Kazoh Kitamori, *Theology of the Pain of God* (Richmond, John Knox Press, 1965), p. 45.

[55] Relton, *Studies in Christian Doctrine,* p. 82.

[56] Kitamori, *op. cit.,* p. 44.

life of God. However, the suffering of Christ was also His joy and His death to sin was also His resurrection to life. Thus, the suffering of God is also His joy in suffering and His death is also the death in Resurrection. In the inner experience of the divine neither suffering is possible without joy nor death is possible without resurrection. In suffering there is joy and in death to sin there is life in resurrection. The Pauline statements that "I rejoice in my suffering" (Colossians 1 : 24) or "Death is swallowed up in victory" (I Corinthians 15 : 54) seem to express this paradox of Christian experience, which is the reflection of God's own experience. God, who is the first and the last, says "I died, and behold I am alive for evermore" (Revelation 1 : 17–18). Again, God is He "who died and came to life" (Revelation 2 : 8). This is the mystery of divine experience in which suffering and joy as well as crucifixion and resurrection are paradoxically united together.[57] In this paradox we repudiate the validity of both the impassibility doctrine and the death-of-God theology.

As to the question of the compatibility of divine impassibility with the reality of the Cross, let us consider it in terms of the *Agape* of the Cross. As we have already stated, the reality of the Cross as the eternal Cross of God in Himself deals primarily with the Christological aspect of Atonement, while the reality of the Cross as the *Agape* of the Cross deals with the Soteriological aspect of Atonement. The *Agape* of the Cross implies the inclusive unity of both the depth of divine love and that of divine passibility. Thus, it is neither the depth of divine love alone nor the divine passibility alone, but the combination of the two which manifests itself as the depth of divine empathy to participate in the world. This inclusive unity of both divine love and divine passibility alone has a saving efficacy, that is, a soteriological aspect of Atonement. In other words, the redemptive love is always love with suffering. Neither love without suffering nor suffering without love is redemptive. "Just as St. Paul believed that our human love cannot be effectively redemptive in the lives of our fellow men unless it is a suffering love, so he believed that the redemptive love of God must in some way also involve suffering."[58] If love is really to be redemptive, it must be a suffering love, that is, the *Agape* of the Cross. *Agape* is not redemptive unless it is also suffering. To deny the suffering of God is to deny the redemptive work of God. "The redemption of

---

[57] After Barth had delivered the Gifford Lectures, he received a letter which indicates that "it is both impossible and incomprehensible that God should suffer death and perdition." Barth's answer was this: "The resurrection is the answer to the impossibility of His death." See *The Knowledge of God and the Service of God According to the Teaching of the Reformation* (London: Hodder and Stoughton, 1938), p. 84, and 86 (notes).

[58] John Baillie, *The Place of Jesus Christ in Modern Christianity* (New York: Charles Scribner's Sons, 1929), p. 52.

evil through suffering includes the suffering of God."[59] If we attribute suffering to the humanity of Christ alone, we may have to give up the idea that the saving efficacy comes from the divine. The impassible God cannot bear the sins of the world. Therefore, the doctrine of divine impassibility leaves us the question Donald Baillie asks, "whether it was really God that suffered, and if not, how we can say that God bore our sins."[60] This is why the reality of the Cross radically rejects any attempt to justify the concept of impassible God. To believe in the doctrine of divine impassibility is quite contrary to the central affirmation of our Christian faith that "God was in Christ reconciling the world to himself."

3. Divine Passibility as the Necessary Consequence of Atonement

We have already stated that the element of vicarious suffering is the indispensable part of God's saving efficacy. In other words, God cannot redeem the world without being involved Himself in suffering. What is, then, the relationship between God's redemptive process and His suffering? This is the question which we intend to examine here.

The redemptive act of God is so closely related to the concept of divine passibility that we cannot really separate one from the other. His redemptive act itself is the act of His suffering, and his suffering is the way of redemption. Suffering is not something which comes as a by-product of redemption but is a necessary ingredient of the redemptive process. Thus, the suffering of God is a necessary consequence of the redemptive activity of God. As Bonhoeffer says, "the endurance of the Cross is not an accidental tragedy, but a necessary suffering."[61] The eternal Cross is not elected in the heart of God because it is beautiful, but because it is the indispensable quality of His redemptive love in the face of the fact of sin and evil. If there was some way to redeem the world other than through Cross-bearing, we certainly believe that God would not have to sacrifice His own Son on the Cross. We believe that He "bears a Cross because it is only by Cross-bearing that the purpose of love can be achieved."[62] Jesus already knew that it was not his own choice but his destiny, which was already decided within the eternal plan of salvation, to suffer and die on the Cross for the redemption of mankind (Matthew 20 : 28; Mark 10 : 45). This was why, when Peter wished to prevent Jesus from going to Jerusalem to suffer and be killed, Jesus said to him, "Get behind me,

[59] Bernard M. Loomer, op. cit., p. 278.
[60] Donald M. Baillie, op. cit., p. 198.
[61] Dietrich Bonhoeffer, The Cost of Discipleship, trans. by R. H. Fuller (New York: The Macmillan Company, 1959), p. 73.
[62] Edgar S. Brightman, Is God a Person? (New York: Association Press, 1932), p. 80.

Satan! You are a hindrance to me; for you are not on the side of God, but of men" (Matthew 16 : 21–23). The suffering of Christ was already prefigured by the prophets. Especially, the "Servant Songs" in Isaiah 53 vividly depict the rejected and afflicted Servant who bears the sin of many. As it is written, Christ *should* suffer and die (Luke 24 : 46). The idea of the necessity for the Cross is found in Acts in Peter's speech (2 : 23; 3 : 18), the Church's prayer (4 : 27, 28), Paul's argument with Jews in Thessalonica (17 : 3) and Paul's defense before King Agrippa (26 : 23). The necessity of suffering for redemption is much vividly expressed in Hebrews 9 : 22: "without the shedding of blood, there is no forgiveness of sins." Therefore, "Suffering and rejection are laid upon Jesus as a divine necessity, and every attempt to prevent it is the work of evil."[63] Divine suffering is not an accidental but the necessary consequence of God's redemptive activity in the world.

In conclusion, we see that Bishop Aulén's so-called "classical idea of the atonement" seems to support our assertion that divine suffering is the necessary consequence of God's redemptive work. The central theme of the classical idea of the atonement is

. . . a divine conflict and victory; Christ—Christus Victor—fights against and triumphs over the evil powers of the world, the "tyrants" under which mankind is in bondage and suffering, and in Him God reconciles the world to Himself.[64]

Even though it presupposes the prescientific notion of mystic and dualistic world views, we cannot deny that it is based on biblical witness.[65] One of the main characteristics of the "classical idea of the atonement" is to conceive redemption from beginning to end as the work of God Himself, a *continuous* divine work, while the objective or the "Latin" type of the atonement begins with God's will and finally is carried out by Christ on behalf of man, and therefore, it is called a *discontinuous* divine work. Furthermore, the subjective or "humanistic" type of atonement no longer regards redemption as the work of God but the work of man. Consequently, the classical idea of atonement alone can understand that "the conflict and triumph of Christ is God's own conflict and triumph it is God who in Christ reconciles the world to Himself."[66] In this conflict and struggle of God to overcome the power of evil, the inner tension between His transcendence and immanence

---

[63] Bonhoeffer, *op. cit.,* p. 76.
[64] Gustaf Aulén, *Christus Victor: An Historical Study of the Three Main Types of the Idea of the Atonement* (London: S. P. C. K., 1931), p. 20.
[65] See especially the Pauline statements of Galatians 4 : 8–10; Colossians 1 : 16; Ephesians 6 : 12; Romans 8 : 38; I Corinthians 2 : 6–8, and others.
[66] Aulén, *op. cit.,* p. 168.

reaches its climax. That is to say that God not only suffers intensively in Christ to overcome the power of evil but suffers continuously as long as there is evil in the world. Thus we can conclude that the classical idea of the atonement is compatible with the idea that divine passibility is a necessary consequence of God's redemptive activity in the world

The Holy Spirit and Divine Passibility

The Holy Spirit is not to be conceived as an attribute of God but God Himself in action. Thus, the passibility of God, which is an attribute of God, is always subsequent to the Holy Spirit. If God is capable of suffering, it is nothing else than the capacity of the Holy Spirit, who is the active presence of the personal God Himself in the world. This is why the concept of divine passibility and that of the Holy Spirit are closely related to each other. Our attempt here is to see exclusively the relationship between them, in order to assert their compatibility to strengthen our thesis that God is passible.

1. Divine Empathy as an Activity of the Holy Spirit

The meaning of the spirit can be traced back to the Hebrew word *"ruach,"* which is translated in Greek *"pneuma."* The word *"pneuma"* literally means "blowing" or "the breathing out of air." The primitive meaning of the spirit is, then, to be understood as the movement of the air.[67] Therefore, by analogy, the Holy Spirit can be conceived as the movement of God into the world. In other words, God reveals Himself in the world because He is also the Holy Spirit. "The Spirit of God in us as much as Immanuel was God with us."[68] Through the activity of the Holy Spirit God moves into the world, not merely confronting men but *participating* in them as fully as to be united together. As Brunner said, "When we say 'Holy Spirit' we mean that mode of God's being by which He is present within us, and operates in our spirit and heart."[69] It is the nature of the Holy Spirit to abide in us (John 14 : 16, 17) and have communion with us (II Corinthians 13 : 14). This movement of the Holy Spirit to participate in the world is to be conceived as the empathy of God. Therefore, the empathy of God is an activity of the Holy Spirit.

The relationship between the empathy of God and the work of the Holy Spirit is well illustrated in the Pauline statement that "God's love has been

[67] Hendrikus Berkhof, *The Doctrine of the Holy Spirit: The Annie Kinkead Warfield Lectures, 1963–1964* (Richmond: John Knox Press, 1964), p. 13.
[68] Harold J. Ockenga, *The Spirit of the Living God* (London: Fleming H. Revell Company, 1947), p. 16
[69] Brunner, *Dogmatics, III*, 12.

poured into our hearts through the Holy Spirit" (Romans 5 : 5). To Paul the empathy of God means the infusion of *Agape* in our hearts. Since God is both love (I John 4 : 8) and Spirit (John 4 : 24), the empathy of God which is a functional mode of *Agape* is an activity of the Holy Spirit. *Agape* and the Holy Spirit are not only united in one but mutually dependent on each other. Neither is *Agape* the self-giving movement of God without the Holy Spirit, nor is the Holy Spirit the redemptive power of God without *Agape*. This inclusive unity and mutual dependency between the Holy Spirit and *Agape* are the bases of our argument that the empathy of God is an activity of the Holy Spirit.

The idea that the empathy of God is an activity of the Holy Spirit is foremost and most perfectly expressed in Godhead. In the inner-trinitarian life of God, the Father is empathically united with the Son and the Son with the Father through the Holy Spirit. It is the activity of the Holy Spirit to unite the Father with the Son. Robinson understands this unifying activity of the Holy Spirit as the "Unifying Center," because the unifying activity of God is centered around the Holy Spirit.[70] This "Unifying Center" is the prototype of divine empathy, which determines all other unifying activities in the world. The prototype of divine empathy is most perfectly manifested in the Incarnation of God in Christ. The New Testament witnesses that the birth of Christ, which is the perfect empathy of God in history, was carried out through the Holy Spirit (Matthew 1 : 18−21). Moreover, this prototype of divine empathy is reflected in human life. If human spirit is a reflection of divine Spirit, the basic category of social unity which is the I-Thou relation in humanity is also a copy of the I-Thou relation in Godhead. Just as human spirit is a reflection of divine unity. Thus, the empathic union of Godhead is the activity of the Holy Spirit, while the empathic union of humanity is the operation of the human spirit. If we call this basic category of social unity, which is the empathic relation of I-Thou in human society, the "sociality" of human spirit, "sociality" is not only the content of the spirit but an essential and inalienable attribute of the spirit.[71] The operation of human spirit as "sociality" is a reflection of the work of the Holy Spirit as the "Unifying Center." However, this basic category of social unity is continuously being broken by our sin and renewed through the coming of the Holy Spirit. Thus, the coming of the Holy Spirit at Pentecost signifies the dramatic expression of the empathic participation of God in the world. It has not abolished the "sociality" of human spirit but has restored its brokenness through the crea-

---

[70] H. Wheeler Robinson, *The Christian Experience of the Holy Spirit* (New York: Harper and Brothers, 1928), p. 68.
[71] *Ibid.*, p. 73.

tion of *koinonia*. *Koinonia* is nothing else than a rebirth of the empathic relation of I-Thou which is the basis of a genuine sociality. Therefore, the adequate understanding of *koinonia* includes the empathic participation of man in God through the Holy Spirit. In this regard, the correct translation of *koinonia* would be the *participation* in the Holy Spirit.[72] A good illustration for this is found in Philippians 2 : 1–2, where *"koinonia pneumatos"* is translated into "participation in the Spirit" according to the Revised Standard Version. As a result, "Most scholars are agreed that the fundamental idea which *koinonia* conveys is that of 'participation in something in which others par-participate.'"[73] *Koinonia* is, then, the community of human participation in the Holy Spirit who becomes the Subject of all those who participate in the community. In other words, *koinonia* is the empathic community in which "the basis social category is the I-Thou relation" and "the Thou of the other is the divine Thou."[74] Therefore, we conclude that the creation of *koinonia* by the Holy Spirit is the clearest existential evidence that the empathy of God is an activity of the Holy Spirit.

2. The Incompability of the Concept of Divine Impassibility with the Empathy of God as an Activity of the Holy Spirit

We have defined the meaning of the Holy Spirit as the mode of God by which He empathically participates in the world, in order to make Himself an existential reality. Thus the empathy of God involves an activity of the Holy Spirit. The relationship between the empathy of God and the work of the Holy Spirit is well illustrated by the Pauline idea of the infusion of *Agape* through the Holy Spirit. This illustration helps us to support the idea that the empathy of God is an activity of the Holy Spirit. The relationship between *Agape* and the Holy Spirit is existentially manifested in *koinonia*. Now, let us examine how the idea of the impassible God is incompatible with the concept of divine empathy as an activity of the Holy Spirit.

If the Holy Spirit means the God of movement and participation in the world, the impassible God is contrary to the very nature of the Holy Spirit. God, who is also the Holy Spirit, cannot be both impassible and dynamic at the same time. To make Him impassible is to negate the dynamic nature of God as the Holy Spirit. Since the Holy Spirit operates as the unifying center of Godhead, the I-Thou relationship which constitutes the basic category

---

[72] Berkhof, *op. cit.,* p. 57.
[73] J. Robert Nelson, *The Realm of Redemption: Studies in the Doctrine of the Nature of the Church in Contemporary Protestant Theology* (London: The Epworth Press, 1951), p. 53.
[74] Dietrich Bonhoeffer, *The Communion of Saints: A Dogmatic Inquiry into the Sociology of the Church* (New York: Harper and Row, 1963), p. 37.

of this unifying center is nothing other than a personal and dynamic relationship. As we have already stated, the traditional doctrine of divine impassibility, which is based on the neo-platonic idea of static ontology, is incompatible with the Biblical idea of the personal and dynamic God.

There are enough evidences in the Scripture to support the idea that the Spirit is regarded as the personal Being, who is capable of experiencing suffering, grief, joy and other emotional life. For example, in Acts the Spirit is known as the person who speaks (1 : 16; 8 : 29; 11 : 12, and others), appoints (20 : 28), sends (13 : 4), witnesses (5 : 32), is tempted (5 : 9) and resisted by the people (7 : 15). Paul also understands the Holy Spirit as the Person who is capable of suffering and grief because of our sins (Ephesians 4 : 30). Thus "the Spirit is described as the 'minister of the suffering.'"[75] If the empathy of God is regarded as the work of the Holy Spirit, who is also "the inward personal present of God,"[76] God cannot be impassible. As a result, the reality of the Holy Spirit as the Person who participates in the world to share the grief and suffering of sinful men is a radical repudiation of any motive to ascribe a concept of divine impassibility.

Paul's idea of the infused love seems to convey a profound insight about the relationship between *Agape* and the Holy Spirit. In other words, the statement, "God's love has been poured into our hearts through the Holy Spirit (Romans 5 : 5), seems to imply that the Holy Spirit is not only identical with *Agape* but an agent through which *Agape* is infused into our hearts. The identity of the Holy Spirit with *Agape* is further demonstrated in the Johannine statements, "God is love" (I John 4 : 8) and "God is Spirit" (John 4 : 24). The Holy Spirit who is the inward personal presence of God is also the *Agape* which is the essence of God Himself. At the same time, the Holy Spirit is the agent of *Agape*. In other words, the Holy Spirit is not only the very nature of *Agape* but the *agent* of it at the same time. This is a paradoxical nature of the Holy Spirit. Since the Holy Spirit is *Agape* which is infused into our hearts through the Holy Spirit itself, the experience of God as *Agape* is nothing other than that of Him as the Holy Spirit. Since we have already demonstrated that God as *Agape* is able to experience suffering in His empathy for the evil of the world, God as the Holy Spirit is also able to experience it. As Brasnett says,

Being a spirit of love the Holy Spirit can be hurt and wounded; being a spirit that works by love and not by force he can be resisted and defined. . . . The anguish of the Holy Spirit at the sin of the world must be a dreadful and awful reality; loving with a

---

[75]   Mozley, *op. cit.,* p. 13.
[76]   Brunner, *Dogmatics, I,* 215.

love great beyond our power to comprehend. He suffers with an equal agony when his love is stayed in beneficience.[77]

Finally, the biblical notion of *koinonia* as the actual manifestation of the Holy Spirit seems to be incompatible with an idea of the impassible God. If *koinonia* is to be understood as the restoration of the broken sociality of human spirit, which is based on the empathic relation of I-Thou in which the Thou is the Holy Spirit, it is nothing less than the empathic community of the I and Thou. In this community, "the I and the Thou are fitted into one another in infinite nearness, in mutual penetration, forever inseparable, resting on one another in inmost mutual participation, feeling and experiencing together, and sustaining the general stream of spiritual interaction."[78] If the Thou of this community is the divine Thou, who is the Holy Spirit, then the inmost mutual penetration and participation of this Thou with the I of suffering humanity make feeling and experiencing together. Thus, the suffering of humanity is also experienced in the Holy Spirit as a result of His empathic penetration in the I as the Thou. As a result it is almost impossible to assert that the Holy Spirit is a mode of an impassible God by which He neither shares nor participates in the community of suffering humanity. We conclude, therefore, that the concepts of *koinonia* and *Agape* illustrate that the idea of the impassible God is quite incompatible with the nature of the Holy Spirit.

3. The Holy Spirit as the Continual Manifestation of Divine Passibility

We have so far dealt with the Holy Spirit in terms of the creative power of God, the giver of life and strength in every activity of God, but we now come to examine a most significant aspect of our concern, that is, the relationship between the Holy Spirit and Jesus Christ in terms of the problem of divine passibility. We may begin with this conviction that, if God ever continues to suffer for our sin, it is none other than the perpetual presence of the suffering God in Christ through the Holy Spirit. In other words, if the Holy Spirit implies the continual manifestation of God's suffering, He must manifest Himself as the perpetual presence of the living Christ, who is the perfection of divine revelation in history. Therefore, the relationship between the Holy Spirit and Jesus Christ leads to the possibility of establishing the relationship between the Holy Spirit and the suffering of God. Let us begin our examination with the relationship between the Holy Spirit and Jesus Christ.

---

[77] Brasnett, *op. cit.,* pp. 60–61.
[78] Bonhoeffer, *The Communion of Saints,* p. 48.

We notice from the New Testament witnesses that there is the double relation between the Holy Spirit and Jesus Christ. The synoptic gospels predominantly depict "Jesus as the bearer of the Spirit."[79] That is to signify the prior existence of the Holy Spirit to the historical revelation of God in Jesus Christ. The priority of the Holy Spirit is well illustrated by the gospels in the following events: the coming of the Holy Spirit at the birth of Jesus (Matthews 1 : 20), the descent of the Holy Spirit like a dove at His baptism (Matthew 3 : 16; cf. Mark 1 : 10; Luke 3 : 22; John 1 : 32), being led by the Holy Spirit to the wilderness (Matthew 4 : 1), casting out demons by the Holy Spirit (Matthew 12 : 28), or the power of Christ to proclaim the good news through the Holy Spirit (Luke 4 : 18). On the other hand, the Johannine and Pauline writings generally point to Jesus Christ as "the sender of the Holy Spirit." Here, in contrast to the synoptic gospels, Jesus Christ becomes prior to the Holy Spirit. The priority of Jesus Christ is found in many incidents. Some of them are to describe the Holy Spirit as the Spirit of Christ (Romans 8 : 9; II Corinthians 3 : 17; Galatians 4 : 6; Philippians 1 : 19), the coming of the Holy Spirit in Christ's name (John 14 : 26) or Christ's explicit statements that the Christ will send the Holy Spirit after His death (John 15 : 26; 16 : 7). However, the double relation between Jesus Christ as the receiver of the Holy Spirit and Him as the sender of the Holy Spirit is by no means contradictory. In fact, they are united together in the witness of John, who says, "I saw the Spirit descend as a dove from heaven, and it remained on him" (John 1 : 32). Both the sending and receiving of the Holy Spirit are inseparably related to the remaining of the Holy Spirit in Christ. Berkhof puts it quite eloquently when he describes, "Jesus can be the sender of the Spirit only because he is first the receiver and the bearer of the Spirit."[80] The *coming* of the Spirit points to the pre-existence of Christ prior to incarnation, while the *remaining* of the Spirit points to the continuing presence of the living Christ even after the crucifixion. The former represents Jesus Christ as the receiver of the Spirit, while the latter represents Jesus Christ as the bearer of the Spirit. Thus, the historical revelation of God in Christ, which points both backward and forward in the history of salvation, is also the objective manifestation of the Holy Spirit. This is why Barth asserts Jesus Christ as "the objective reality of revelation"[81] and the Holy Spirit as "the subjective reality of revelation."[82] The Holy Spirit, who remains even after the death of Christ, confines Himself to the objective reality of revelation (John 14 : 16;

---

[79] Berkhof, *op. cit.*, p. 17.
[80] *Ibid.*, p. 18.
[81] Barth, *Church Dogmatics, I/2,* 25 ff.
[82] *Ibid.*, p. 203 ff.

15 : 26–27; 16 : 7–11, 13). Therefore, the objective and historical revelation of God in Christ is also the subjective and inward revelation of God through the Holy Spirit. To say it in another way, "through the Holy Spirit Christ Himself, as 'Christ-for-us,' becomes 'Christ-in-us.'"[83] The Holy Spirit is, as Barth says, "no other than the presence and action of Jesus Christ Himself; His stretched out arm; He Himself in the power of His resurrection, i.e., in the power of His revelation as it begins in and with the power of His resurrection and continues to work from this point."[84] The continual presence of the Holy Spirit does not mean the mere extension of the earthly existence of Christ but "it is a matter of the fresh coming of the One who came before. Always and in different ways it is a matter of the coming again of Jesus Christ."[85] In other words, the Holy Spirit means that the Jesus Christ of yesterday freshly becomes the Jesus Christ of today. In this way the suffering of God in Christ yesterday becomes the suffering of God today in the Holy Spirit. The Holy Spirit is also the Jesus Christ of tomorrow, because it is the movement from Christ to the consummation. Thus, the Holy Spirit implies also the fresh coming of the suffering God in Christ again and again until the consummation of God's Kingdom.

The suffering of God in Christ was not terminated at Easter, but it continues to manifest itself through a fresh coming of Christ by the presence of the Holy Spirit.

When He came again in the Easter event, having crossed the frontier of death imposed on all creatures, He did not appear to His disciples as another and purely divine being, but as the one who had come before and lived among them and died on Golgotha.[86]

The testimony of Paul also witnesses the same; when Paul at his conversion heard the voice of the risen Christ, who had said, "I am Jesus, whom you are persecuting" (Acts 9 : 5), "there is the idea that Christ still suffers at the hands of men though his historical passion is past and over."[87] Perhaps the suffering of God which is manifested by the presence of the Holy Spirit may be regarded as the fresh coming of God's suffering in Christ, because the reason for His suffering is fundamentally the same, that is, man's unwillingness to participate in His participation. The participation of Divine Spirit in the whole of men in spite of their rejection of it is in fact His "long-patience" in waiting for their voluntary participation in His participation. This "long-patience" of God signifies the inward experience of divine suffering. As long as men refuse to

[83] Brunner, *Dogmatics, I,* 215.
[84] Barth, *Church Dogmatics, IV/2,* 322–323.
[85] Barth, *Church Dogmatics, IV/3,* 293
[86] *Ibid.,* p. 357.
[87] Donald M. Baillie, *op. cit.,* p. 194.

participate in divine participation, the suffering of God will continue in the presence of the Holy Spirit. This is why the presence of the Holy Spirit in the midst of the evil of the world implies the continual manifestation of divine passibility.

The Trinity and Divine Passibility

As we have already examined in the previous chapter, it was the trinitarian issue which gave a rise to the problem of divine passibility. Our investigation in this chapter is to be concluded with that very same problem which gave it a start. The trinitarian issue is so complex that our intention here is merely to point out the significance of this doctrine in relation to the concept of divine passibility. Thus, let us first look at the doctrine in terms of divine empathy. We don't here intend to give an answer to the trinitarian issue but to provide an alternative approach to the trinitarian problem. Secondly, the compatibility of the concept of divine impassibility is to be tested in terms of the alternative position we have taken. Finally, a brief summary on the concept of divine passibility is to be stated in the light of our trinitarian thinking.

1. The Inner-trinitarian Life as the Prototype of Divine Empathy

The doctrine of the Trinity, which has been accepted by the Church, concerns itself primarily with the inner-trinitarian life of God. Even though it is still disputable as to whether the concept of trinitarian God has a sound biblical foundation or not, there are enough biblical passages to point in the direction of the doctrine of the Trinity.[88] For instance, the Spirit is to be both the Spirit of God and that of the Son (Galatians 4 : 6) or of Jesus (Acts 16 : 7). In Romans 8 : 9–11 the Spirit of God and of Christ are the same and one Spirit. There is the unity of the Son and the Father (John 10 : 30; 17 : 11, 22, and others). In II Thessalonians 2 : 13–14 and I Corinthians 12 : 4–6, God, Christ and the Spirit are at the forefront of Paul's thinking. Besides these examples, there are ample evidences to support the presence of this threefold pattern especially in Paul's mind (II Corinthians 3 : 3; Romans 14 : 17–18; 15 : 16, 30; Philippians 3 : 3; Colossians 1 : 6–8, and others). Consequently, Richardson is right to assert that "The New Testament formulates no doctrine of the Trinity, but its threefold doxological and liturgical formulae (e.g., Matthew

---

[88] This position is taken by Emil Brunner in his *Dogmatics, I,* p. 217. On the other hand, Karl Barth has taken a definite position that the doctrine is directly rooted in the biblical witness. "Therefore," Barth said, "the revelation itself attested by Scripture we call 'the root of the doctrine of the Trinity.'" Barth, *Church Dogmatics, I/I,* 353.

28 : 19; II Corinthians 1 : 21ff; 13 : 14; I Peter 1 : 2; Jude 20ff; Revelation 1 : 4–6) sufficiently demonstrate that the Apostolic Church worshipped one God in Trinity and Trinity in unity."[89] For the sake of convenience, Barth's understanding of the doctrine is used as a norm of our working definition.

By the doctrine of the Trinity we understand the Church doctrine concerning the oneness of God in the three modes of existence of Father, Son and the Holy Spirit or concerning the three-fold otherness of the one God in the modes of existence of Father, Son and the Holy Spirit. All that had . . . to be expounded here in deatil, could and can only be an exposition of the oneness in threeness and the threeness in oneness of God.[90]

In exploring the idea of the "oneness in threeness" and the "threeness in oneness" of God, we may begin with the essential nature of God, which we have already defined as holy love or *Agape*. The statements in I John 4 : 8, 16, 19, help us to conceive the God is eternally love prior to, and independent of His love for us. This indicates that God's love for us is subsequent to His love in His inner-trinitarian life from all eternity. This *Agape* with which the Father loves the Son and the Son loves the Father even before the foundation of the world (John 17 : 24) is to be understood as the prototype of Christian love which we experience in life. As Barth said, "In God Himself it is the love of the Father to the Son, of the Son to the Father. This eternal *love in God Himself* is the Holy Spirit."[91] This prototype of *Agape,* which unites the Father with the Son and the Son with the Father in the Holy Spirit, is the ontological foundation of the Trinity.

Since the prototype of *Agape,* that is, *Agape* in God Himself, is the Holy Spirit, the inner-trinitarian life of God is to be conceived as the activity of the Holy Spirit in terms of the perfect empathy. In other words, the Trinity is the empathic movement of the Holy Spirit from the Father to the Son and the Son to the Father. As Berkhof said, God's inner-trinitarian relationship means "a great movement, the movement of God as Spirit, moving toward the Son and out of the Son."[92] However, it is important to state that this great movement of God as Spirit in Himself takes place in the most perfect and original mode of divine empathy. This movement of God as the Holy Spirit, that is, the activity of the prototype of *Agape,* originally and perfectly takes place in Godhead prior to our experience in life. That is to say that the historical revelation of God in Christ presupposes the empathic movement of God as

[89]   Cyril C. Richardson, *The Doctrine of the Trinity* (New York: The Abingdon Press, 1958), p. 122.
[90]   Barth, *Church Dogmatics, I/l,* 431.
[91]   Barth, *Credo* (New York: Charles Scribner's Sons, 1962), p. 136.
[92]   Berkhof, *op. cit.,* p. 116.

the Spirit in the inner-trinitarian life of Himself. Therefore, God's movement in history is to be understood as the re-enactment of the inner-trinitarian movement of God as the Holy Spirit.

As we have already suggested, there are three distinctive movements of God as the Holy Spirit in Godhead: the *receiving* of God as the Holy Spirit from the Father to the Son, the *remaining* of God as the Holy Spirit in the Son,[93] and the *sending* of God as the Holy Spirit from the Son to the Father.[94] The first inner-trinitarian movement of divine empathy is re-enacted in the incarnation of God in Christ. The second inner-trinitarian movement of it is re-enacted in the life and death of Jesus Christ. Finally, the third inner-trinitarian movement is re-enacted in the coming of the Paraclete at Pentecost. Thus the activities of receiving, remaining nad sending originally take place in Godhead and come to us as Christian experiences of new birth, new life and hope in Christ. These original activities in Godhead are to be understood as the archetypes of divine empathy, because all other empathic movements of God in history are conditioned by the activities in Godhead. The archetype of divine empathy is often expressed in the Scripture by the single proposition "in." "... Father, art in me, and I in thee" (John 17 : 21) are Jesus' own words. Relton calls this mutual participation as the "Perfect Fellowship" through "the mutual indwelling of the Three in One and One in Three."[95] Baillie also expresses a similar view on the Trinity as the prototype of divine indwelling in us: "The New Testament can also speak of God the Father dwelling in Christ, and of the Holy Spirit given to Christ; and it can speak of God the Father dwelling in us as we in Him, and of Christ dwelling in us, and we in Him."[96] Even though the word "indwelling" has a biblical significance, to describe the inner-trinitarian relationship of God in terms of "mutual indwelling" is quite misleading. The life of mutual indwelling is incompatible with the essence of God, whose loving nature is not to dwell in others but to give Himself to others. Moreover, the concept of "indwelling" can easily lead to the false idea that, for example, God merely dwelt in Jesus Christ rather than that Jesus Christ was really God and man in his experience. Paul's experience that "it is not I who lives, but Christ lives in me" (Galatians 2 : 20) seems to allude to the indwelling experience of Christ in his heart. Nevertheless, the reality of Paul's experience seems to

---

[93] The concept of "the receiving of God as the Holy Spirit from the Father to the Son" is primarily found in the Synoptic Gospels: Matthew 1 : 20; 4 : 1; 12 : 28; Luke 4 : 14, and others. The concept of "the remaining of God as the Holy Spirit in the Son" is primarily found in the Pauline Statements: II Corinthians 3 : 17; Romans 8 : 9–11; Galatians 2 : 20, and others.
[94] Primarily found in the Johannine statements: John 14 : 26, 15 : 26, 16 : 7; and others.
[95] Relton, *Studies in Christian Doctrine,* pp. 45, 46, 179.
[96] Donald M. Baillie, *op. cit.,* p. 147.

be the experience of his self-giving at all costs, even at the unity of himself with Christ's crucifixion and resurrection. This is why Paul begins the statement with "I have been crucified with Christ," before he says "it is not I who lives, but Christ lives in me." Therefore, we ought not to conceive the inner-trinitarian life of God in terms of the fellowship through mutual indwelling. The meaning of the Trinity is, consequently, neither the mutual indwelling of the one in three or three in one nor a mere identity of essence, but it is "the mutual and external self-giving of each person to each other 'person,' it is the movement of each 'toward' the other, the merging of each [experience] 'in' the other without losing separate identity."[97] This dynamic movement of the eternal and complete self-giving of each toward the other to be one in experience is precisely the empathic movement of God in His inner-trinitarian life. In other words, the real meaning of the Trinity is simply the original modes of divine empathy, which means the complete self-giving movement of each feeling to penetrate himself totally into the other, as to be really one experience, without becoming other than himself. The mystery of the Trinity is based on the paradox of divine empathy, that is, each *comes* to *be* or "be-comes" the other in experience without "becoming" other than himself. Therefore, the "receiving," "remaining" and "sending" of God as the Holy Spirit presupposes the archetypal modes of divine empathy in the inner-trinitarian life of God. In the Trinity, the Father, Son and the Holy Spirit are mutually and *perfectly* participating in each other in such a totally self-giving experience as to be one God, who also manifests Himself in three modes of divine empathy. This is why we can call the Trinity the prototype of divine empathy.

The doctrine of the Trinity as the archetype of divine empathy means, on the one hand, a denial of subordinationalism, because it does not make any mode less than the other in Godhead. In the complete giving of their total selves to each other they mutually participate perfectly, so as to be one without losing their self-identity. Therefore, in the modes of divine empathy neither the Son is less than the Father nor the Holy Spirit less than the Son. The archetype of divine empathy means, on the other hand, the denial of modalism, because it does not transform any mode into another mode of divine empathy. Even though they mutually feel into themselves so totally and completely as to be one, they always retain their separate and distinctive identities to be their own modes. Therefore, by the Trinity as the archetype of divine empathy we mean the denial of both subordinationism and modal-

[97] Kenneth J. Foreman, *Identification: Human and Divine* (Richmond: John Knox Press, 1963), p. 78.

ism. Consequently, the doctrine of the Trinity seems adequate to be described as the threefold divine mode of empathy.

2. The Incompatibility of the Concept of Divine Impassibility with the Idea of the Trinity as the Archetype of Divine Empathy

In the previous chapter we have not only surveyed the rise of anti-patripassianism, which was in fact the initial development of the doctrine of divine impassibility by the Church, but repudiated the validity of the anti-patripassian claims in the light of trinitarian thinking. The defense of the early Fathers, especially Tertullian and Hippolytus, over against the patripassian heresy, which was a nickname for the Modalistic Monarchianism, was primarily based on a sharp distinction of persons in the Trinity. As a result of our investigation, we have concluded that the sound doctrine of Trinity asserts neither the transformation of one from the other nor too sharp a distinction among them to hinder a mutual participation. Thus, it repudiates both the patripassian heresy which asserts the unity of Godhead without distinction, and the anti-patripassians who claim the distinctions of persons without a genuine unity. Since we have also postulated that the inner-trinitarian life of God is the archetype of divine empathy, in which the Father, Son and the Holy Spirit are mutually and eternally united together even as to be One without losing their identity, the concept of divine im passibility or the anti-patripassian claim, that the distinctions of divine persons are intended as a safeguard against any ascription of divine passibility, is certainly incompatible with the doctrine of the Trinity as we have defined it. Therefore, we have reassured the incompatibility of the concept of divine impassibility with the sound doctrine of the Trinity.

If the doctrine of the Trinity implies the inner-trinitarian life of God, which is the presupposition of all the activities of God in and for the world, we are led to believe that the sufferings of God with us or on account of us, especially the suffering of God in Christ, are only the reflections of the prototype of divine suffering in Godhead. In other words, "The sorrow (of the Son of God) which openly or secretly fills the heart of man is primarily in the heart of God."[98] In this respect, we have repudiated again and again the idea that the suffering of God is a consequence of the suffering and sin of the world. The *possibility* of tragedy and suffering has been already experienced within the divine life itself, before the fall of man, when man is created to be a free creature. This is to say that the actualization of divine grace implies

---

[98]   Barth, *Church Dogmatics, IV/2*, 225.

both the self-limitation of God and the freedom of man, which includes the potentiality of tragedy and suffering. The self-limitation of God and the potentiality of His suffering have already come into being at the time of creation. Therefore, it is not a bit of a surprise to know that Brightman has postulated the finite God in terms of "the Given," which is "a limitation within the divine nature."[99] He presents the constant struggle and suffering of divine life itself in order to overcome and control this irrational nature of the "Given" which is the source of eternal problems and suffering for God. This idea of divine suffering in the inner life of God is also clearly echoed by Tillich's idea of the divine life as a struggle for the eternal conquest of the negative.[100] God's suffering is not something which comes from His response to human sufferings, but He has been involved in His own suffering even much before the tragedy of man in history. The significance of the inner-trinitarian life of God as the prototype of divine empathy lies in this, that all the experiences of tragedy and suffering between God and man in the world must be anticipated in the inner community of the Father, Son and the Holy Spirit. This is why Barth said, "it was first and supremely in Himself that the conflict between Himself and this man, and the affliction which threatened this man, were experienced and borne."[101] Thus, the suffering of Jesus Christ was first and originally experienced within the inner life of God before the coming of God in Christ. The suffering of God before the coming of Christ in the world is in fact the suffering of God as the Father. Thus, as Barth said, "there is a *particula veri* in the teaching of the early Patripassians."[102] The denial of the suffering of the Father in spite of the suffering of His Son is also the denial of the intimate relationship between the Father and the Son through the Holy Spirit. If we believe that the Father, Son and the Holy Spirit are so completely and perfectly participating in one another as to be one in experience, the suffering of Christ ought to be the suffering of the Father and the Holy Spirit as well. "In Jesus Christ," Barth again said, "God Himself, the God who is the one true God, the Father with the Son in the unity of the Spirit, has suffered what it befell this man to suffer to the bitter end."[103] To say it simply, the suffering of Jesus Christ was the suffering of the triune God Himself. Therefore, we must radically repudiate the doctrine of impassibility in the light of the divine Trinity as the archetype of divine empathy. The doctrine of impassibility is, then, an almost impossible idea to be held from the standpoint of the view of the Trinity.

[99] Edgar S. Brightman, *The Problem of God* (New York: The Abingdon Press, 1930), p. 183.
[100] Tillich, *Systematic Theology, III,* 405.
[101] Barth, *Church Dogmatics, IV/3,* 414.
[102] Barth, *Church Dogmatics, III/2,* 357.
[103] Barth, *Church Dogmatics, IV/3,* 414.

3. The Trinity as the Integral Reality of Divine Passibility

The inner-trinitarian life of God can be understood as the integral reality of divine manifestations. If the Holy Spirit is "the inclusive symbol for the divine life,"[104] the Trinity is the integral symbol for the inner life of God, who is neither totally transcendent only nor totally immament only, but both totally transcendent and immanent at the same time. The failure to maintain the creative tension between the transcendence (or the ultimate) and the immanent (or the concrete) would result in the danger of falling into Tritheism or Unitarianism.[105] In other words, the Trinity is the integral symbol of the dialectical correlation between Tritheism and Unitarianism, that is, the paradoxical unity of experience between the divine plurality and singularity. This is why the integral reality of divine life does not consist of the uniformity of the similarities but the correlative unity of the dissimilarities. The Trinity is the integral reality for the divine life because these dissimilar members— the Father, the Son and the Holy Spirit are so empathically integrated that they are one God. Nevertheless, no one member is dispensable for the integrality of the whole community of the inner divine life. That means that God the Father is not really the Father without the Son, who is also not really the Son without the Father. The same is true of the Holy Spirit. In order to illustrate this empathic integration of divine life, let us consider the Pauline analogy of "the body of Christ" (I Corinthians 12) as the reflection of the integral life of the inner-trinitarian community. In the body of Christ many members who are dissimilar are united to make one Body of Christ (I Corinthians 12 : 12) and each member is indispensable for the integrality of the whole (I Corinthians 12 : 22–23). Moreover, "if one member suffers, all suffer together (I Corinthians 12 : 26). If this analogy could be applied to the inner-trinitarian community, which is the original and primary community of all other communities, we are readily led to believe that the suffering of one person in the Trinity is eventually the suffering of the whole community of inner divine life. Therefore, the Trinity is the integral reality of divine passibility.

Let us now apply the Pauline analogy of the body of Christ in order to understand the suffering relationship among the members of divine life itself. According to Paul's analogy, the community of believers, which is the body of Christ, is very much like a physical body which represents the most perfect form of integrality in our experience. Since the community of inner divine life is the most original and perfect form of integral community, we are

---

[104] Tillich, *Systematic Theology, I,* 250.
[105] Tillich, *Systematic Theology, III,* 284.

led to believe that, first of all, the cause for the suffering of one member is intimately related to the cause for the suffering of another member in the inner divine community. If the cause for the suffering of the Father is in the act of His creation, it is intimately related to that of the Son in the act of reconciliation. In other words, creation presupposes reconciliation, and reconciliation presupposes redemption. In this respect, the suffering of the Father presupposes the suffering of the Son and that of the Son presupposes that of the Holy Spirit. The suffering of the Father in sending His only Son is immediately related to the suffering of the Son on the Cross. As Kitamori said, "The words 'the Father begets the Son' are secondary to the primary words 'the Father causes His son to die.'"[106] In other words, the incarnation presupposes the crucifixion of the Son on the Cross. Therefore, the causes for divine suffering are mutually dependent and irrevocally interrelated together.

Secondly, in the perfect form of inner divine community, we can conceive that the suffering of one member is also the suffering of all members in the community. As we have already illustrated from Paul's statement that "if one member suffers, all suffer together," the failure to understand the divine sensitivity to share the mutual experiences among them has resulted in the Church prescribing the impossible doctrine of divine impassibility. Paul's analogy of the Body of Christ has clearly demonstrated that within the body of inner-trinitarian community there must be even more intensively the sharing of their mutual experience in suffering and sorrow. To deny it is to deny the empathic unity of the Trinity. The suffering of one is in fact the suffering of the body of the community in which he is a member. Therefore, anyone who is in or is the Body must suffer together. Consequently, "what Christ felt, did, suffered, was in the truest sense felt, done, suffered by God."[107]

Finally, the integral reality of divine passibility means that in the inner-trinitarian life they not only mutually share the experiences of suffering, sorrow and grief but also they share them *equally*. In other words, the intensity of their suffering is equal, even though each may take a different form of suffering. The intensity of vicarious suffering is measured by its degree of sacrifice, and the degree of sacrifice is relative to the depth of *Agape*. Therefore, if the intensity of divine suffering is measured by the depth of *Agape*, which is the essence of God, and the divine modes of empathy are equally united in this essence of God, we cannot say, unless we believe in subordinationism, that one suffers more or less than the other. In the perfect empathy of Godhead the suffering of one penetrates totally into other

---

[106]   Kitamori, *op. cit.*, p. 47.
[107]   Robinson, *Suffering, Human and Divine,* p. 184; originally quoted from H. R. Mackintosh, *Some Aspects of Christian Belief,* p. 93.

members of divine community. However, the forms of their suffering might be manifested differently. For example, it is very difficult for us to believe that the Father had suffered and died on the Cross, even though the intensity and the nature of His suffering experience was identical with that of Jesus' suffering and death on the Cross. Furthermore, it is beyond our comprehension to believe that the Holy Spirit can experience the physical pain that Jesus bore. Thus each mode of God's presence may manifest into a different form of suffering but is the same suffering. To sum up, the Trinity is the integral reality of divine passibility, because three "persons" in the inner-trinitarian community are so intimately felt to each other that they not only equally experience suffering but mutually share the same goal, that is, the redemption of the world. The God who suffers for us is also the God of Trinity. Therefore, "The view that God Suffers is the recovery of a genuine and important note in the biblical understanding of God. It is thoroughly compatible with Trinitarianism and enriches our understanding of love that binds the 'persons' of the Trinity to each other."[108]

---

[108] William J. Wolf, *No Cross, No Crown: A Study of the Atonement* (New York: Doubleday, 1957), p. 197.

CHAPTER IV

AN APPLICATION OF DIVINE PASSIBILITY:
THE OVERCOMING OF OUR SUFFERING IN THE
FELLOWSHIP OF DIVINE AND HUMAN SUFFERING

One of the soul-searching questions in our generation is much more than mere intellectual curiostiy about the understanding of divine passibility. A meaningful question for suffering humanity in our time may have to do with our honest attempt to relate the concept of divine passibility to our existential situation. Let us, therefore, examine the relevance of divine passibility to the problem of human suffering.

A significant lesson we have learned from this study is the way in which God deals with the problem of suffering in the world. God's way is not to escape the reality of suffering, which is the approach of Secularism but to overcome it through His own suffering. The reality of pain, which has to do with a bodily sensation, can be eliminated through the use of medical science and technology, but the reality of suffering, which has to do with a mutual relationship, cannot be eliminated. The elimination of suffering is eventually the elimination of the reality of life, since relationship is one of life's inevitables for everyone. Therefore, God does not eliminate the reality of suffering but bears it in order to overcome our suffering with His suffering. Likewise, the Christian answer to suffering is not to avoid it but to bear it in the right way, that is, to participate in God's suffering with our suffering. Through our participation in His suffering with our suffering, our suffering may be like the suffering of Christ, who has endured the depth of human suffering through His fellowship with the Father. Certainly, Christ suffered "not that men might not suffer but that their suffering might be like his."[1] In other words, the Christian answer to the problem of human suffering is not to avoid but to bear it in a right way.

If the answer is the overcoming of suffering through our participation in divine suffering with our suffering, we must resolve several questions in relation to this answer. How can we participate in divine suffering with our our suffering? What do we mean to participate in divine suffering with our

---

[1] Margaret E. Rose, ed., *The Problem of Suffering: A Collection of Essays Based on a Series of Broadcast Talks for Sixth Forms, Provided by the B. B. C. Under the General Title "The Christian Religion and Its Philosophy,"*(The British Broadcasting Corporation, 1962), p. 12.

suffering? How can we overcome suffering in our participation in divine suffering? What is the fruit of being overcome in our suffering in divine suffering? Let us attempt to deal with the first two questions with "The fellowship of divine and human suffering," and the last two question with "Overcoming human suffering in divine suffering."

The Fellowship of Divine and Human Suffering

The first question which we are going to answer is this: How can we participate in divine suffering with our suffering? Since this question presupposes a prior coming of God in our suffering, let us first examine the nature of divine participation in our suffering.

As we have already indicated, it is the very nature of *Agape,* the essence of divine nature, to take the form of divine empathy to come into being with us. This empathic participation of divine love manifests itself as divine suffering due to our sin and evil in the world. Thus, we can conceive that God has already participated in our suffering even before we ever come to realize the pain in our body. Because God has already participated in our suffering, we become the objects of "His own participation, His care, His suffering."[2] As the objects of God's participating suffering, we are utterly dependent on Him, even though we are often insensitive to His participation in our suffering. Paul expresses divine participation in our suffering in terms of *Agape,* on which all forms of our suffering such as tribulation, distress, persecution, famine, nakedness, and so forth, are inescapably dependent (Romans 8 : 35ff). Because God participates in our suffering, our suffering can be regarded "as a suffering with Him" and "in His Fellowship."[3] Moreover, because our suffering is in His suffering, we can go to the suffering God who is "poor, scorned, without shelter and bread and consumed by sin, weakness and death."[4] Thus, "to be called into the fellowship of God is to be called into the fellowship of that suffering for sin."[5] God's invitation is then extended to us in the fellowship of bearing the cross (Mark 8 : 34), sharing the bitter cup (Mark 10 : 38) and being crucified with Christ (Galatians 2 : 20). To participate in divine suffering with our suffering means precisely to accept this invitation to be in the fellowship of suffering.

If our participation in divine suffering with our suffering means to accept

---

[2] Barth, *Church Dogmatics, II/1,* 373.

[3] Barth, *Church Dogmatics, IV/2,* 611.

[4] J. Robert Nelson, "Tolerance, Bigotry and the Christian Faith," *Religion in Life* (Autumn, 1964), p. 556. See also Bonhoeffer, *Prisoner of God,* p. 167.

[5] H. Wheeler Robinson, *The Cross in the Old Testament* (London: S. C. M. Press, 1955), p. 192.

God's call to be in the fellowship of suffering, how can we accept that invitation? It is not our arrogance and pride to avoid our suffering as a by-product of human ignorance, but our courage of faith to accept it as the "trans-rational" reality which can be overcome only through this fellowship of divine and human suffering. In other words, it is not the arrogance of our reason but the venture of our faith which makes us to participate in His suffering with our suffering. Dietrich Bonhoeffer illustrates it very well when he says:

It is in such a life that we throw ourselves utterly in the arms of God and participate in His sufferings in the world and watch with Christ in Gethsemane. That is faith that is *Metancia,* and that is what makes a man a Christian (cf. Jeremiah 45). How can success make us arrogant or failure lead us astray, when we participate in the sufferings of God by living in this world?[6]

There are notable attempts in the Old Testament, especially in Habakkuk, Psalms 73 and Job, to solve the problem of suffering. Nevertheless, as Hooker says, none of them is able to find a logical answer to the problem, but they find their satisfaction in trust in God.[7] The New Testament answer to the problem of suffering is the Cross, which transcends all the logical protests against the great and unjust sufferings in the world. It is the act of sheer faith and trust to accept the Cross, which is the most embracing symbol of divine invitation for us to participate in His suffering. This is why to take up the Cross and follow Christ (Matthew 16 : 24) is in fact to participate in His suffering with our suffering. In faith our suffering and the suffering of the crucified are united together,[8] and the former is embraced by the latter. In faith our suffering is grasped by the presence of divine suffering. At the same time, in suffering God and man meet together, for faith includes the element of suffering. Faith is not really faith if it is not suffering, as the real *Agape* is the suffering love. Faith in God sustains us to overcome suffering, while suffering through the Holy Spirit trains the unquenchable faith. This faith is our active response to the divine decision, that is, the divine participation to be our subject in our suffering. Therefore, faith emancipates us from suffering *alone* to be suffering *with.* This is to say that in faith we who are the subject of our suffering become the object of His suffering. This transition from the subject to the object of His suffering implies precisely our participating suffering with our suffering.

Our participation in divine suffering with our suffering, that is, the transition from the subject of our suffering to the object of His suffering, means "a

---

[6] Dietrich Bonhoeffer, *Prisoner for God: Letters and Papers from Prison,* trans. by R. H. Fuller (New York: The Macmillan Company, 1954), p. 169.

[7] Morna D. Hooker, *Jesus and the Servant: The Influence of the Concept of Deutero-Isaiah in the New Testament* (London: S. P. C. K., 1959), p. 140.

[8] Brunner, *Dogmatics, II,* 182.

transformation of meaning," the transformation from the meaninglessness to the meaningfulness of our suffering. The participation of our suffering in divine suffering alone makes the transition from the involuntary suffering to voluntary suffering and from the penal suffering to the vicarious suffering. In other words, in our participation in the empathic suffering of God, our suffering due to us for our sins is, as Robinson said, "taken up into the purpose of grace, and penalty becomes vicarious suffering."[9] In the process of this transition, man is brought to himself and becomes a real man. "To be a [real] man means to be so situated in God's presence as Jesus is, that is, to be the Bearer of the Wrath of God."[10] When man's real self is clearly disclosed, he can have a genuine fellowship with the suffering God. As Barth has stated, "There in the depths of his naked and true reality God is His Neighbour and Brother suffering with him and for him."[11] This naked and true man is not a "religious" man but simply "a man" who is a Christian. In other words,

To be a Christian does not mean to be religious in a particular way, to cultivate some particular form of ascetism (as a sinner, a penitent or a saint), but to be a man. It is not some religious act which makes a Christian what he is, but participation in the suffering of God in the life of the world.[12]

This is why "Man is challenged to participate in the suffering of God at the hands of a godless world."[13] Bonhoeffer not only believed that the participation in the suffering of God is the distinctive mark of a Christian, but also lived with the idea that God Himself shared his suffering in the hours of his grieving. As Leibholz has said, "Bonhoeffer's standing with God in his hour of grieving explains, ultimately, why he did not take his own suffering seriously and why his courage was so great and uncompromising."[14] His courage to go through that uncompromising suffering was in fact the unbroken fellowship between his suffering and divine suffering.

The fellowship of divine and human suffering is expressed in a concrete form, that is, the Body of Christ which is "the fellowship of the Cross, participation in the suffering and glory of Christ."[15] Albert Schweitzer calls the

---

[9] H. Wheeler Robinson, *Suffering, Human and Divine* (New York: The Macmillan Company, 1939), p. 183.

[10] Karl Barth, *Dogmatics in Outline* (London: S. C. M. Press, 1949), p. 107.

[11] Barth, *Church Dogmatics, IV/3,* 416.

[12] Bonhoeffer, *Prisoner for God,* p. 166.

[13] *Ibid.*

[14] Dietrich Bonhoeffer, *The Cost of Discipleship,* trans. by R. H. Fuller (New York: The Macmillan Company, 1959), p. 20.

[15] *Ibid.,* p. 187.

Church as "the fellowship of those who bear the mark of pain."[16] The Church as the fellowship of suffering means for Paul to carry the death of Jesus:

We are afflicted in every way, . . . always carrying in the body the death of Jesus, so that the life of Jesus may also be manifested in our bodies. For while we live we are always being given up to death for Jesus' sake, so that the life of Jesus may be manifested in our mortal flesh. So death is at work in us, but life in you (II Corinthians 4 : 8−12).

The sacraments are also regarded as the fellowship of our participation in the body and the blood of Christ (I Corinthians 10 : 16). The Church as the fellowship of suffering is not an accidental outcome but a necessary condition of being of the Body of Christ. It is necessary, for the suffering of Christ, which is not yet exhausted, needs to be completed on behalf of the Church which is the Body of Christ (Colossians 1 : 24). In the Body of Christ there is a continuation of the suffering which Christ has already suffered. Although the necessary suffering is fulfilled by Christ for our redemption, His suffering on earth is continuing through the Church which is His Body. As Bonhoeffer said, "In this grace, Christ has left a 'residue' of suffering for the benefit of His Church, and those who share in this suffering live the very life of Christ, who wills to be formed in his members."[17] Nevertheless, it is a tragic reality of present-day institutional Christianity that makes the Church a symbol of comfort without the fellowship of cross-bearing together, which alone provides the closest communion between God and men. The fellowship of suffering is an essential part of being the Church of Christ, and without it the fellowship of comfort is not possible. Therefore, Paul said, For as we share abundantly in Christ's sufferings, so through Christ we share abundantly in comfort too" (II Corinthians 1 : 5).

To sum up, the fellowship of divine and human suffering is possible only because of the loving God who first comes into the world to share suffering with us, but the fellowship completes itself in our responsive participation in divine suffering through faith. Our participation in divine suffering with our suffering implies the transition from a penalty to a vicarious suffering, that is, from a general to a redemptive suffering, in the realm of the Church.

Overcoming Human Suffering in Divine Suffering

The attempts we have made so far are to answer the first two questions which are implicit in the fellowship of divine and human suffering. We may

---

[16]   Albert Schweitzer, *Out of My Life and Thought: An Autobiography*, trans. by C. T. Champion (New York: H. Holt and Company, 1933), p. 227; see also Ferré, *Evil and the Christian Faith*, p. 75.
[17]   Bonhoeffer, *The Cost of Discipleship*, p. 187.

now deal with the last two questions which have to do with the overcoming of our suffering in divine suffering. If we restate the last two questions, they are as follows: How is our suffering overcome in divine suffering? What is the fruit of being overcome in our suffering in divine suffering? The former question is concerned with the way in which our suffering is overcome, and the latter with the meaning and goal of the overcoming.

How can we overcome our suffering in divine suffering? This question can be answered only on the basis of the fellowship of divine and human suffering. The overcoming of our suffering is possible only in that the fellowship of divine and human suffering produces the following factors: the *meaning* of the positive significance of our suffering, *strength* to endure our suffering, and *hope* to anticipate in the joy of eternal life. These three, meaning, strength and hope, are indispensable to the overcoming of our suffering in divine suffering.

First of all, the fellowship of divine and human suffering gives new meaning and positive significance to our suffering. If the fellowship of divine and human suffering implies the transition from a general to a redemptive suffering (or from a penal to a vicarious suffering), it also signifies the transformation of meaningless suffering to meaningful suffering. Our suffering becomes meaningful because it is related to the divine purpose and activity in our fellow-suffering with God. The meaning becomes real in our experience of suffering because of our conviction that God continues to suffer with us, in spite of our constant failure to participate in His suffering. The positive significance of our suffering is based on the assurance that all our suffering is virtually a part of those of God Himself,[18] because our suffering is empathically united with divine suffering. In the empathic unity between divine and human suffering, our suffering becomes a part of God's redemptive suffering to complete on our part that which is lacking of the afflictions of Christ for the sake of His body which is the Church (Colossians 1 : 24). In other words, in the fellowship of divine and human sufferings "all our suffering gains a positive significance."[19] The negative character of our suffering is transformed into the positive and fruitful means of God's redemptive purpose in the world. This transformation is very significant in the sphere of human experience, because, as Brunner said, "without fostering a desire for suffering, suffering becomes a positive instead of a negative principle."[20] If we are able to see the positive significance in our suffering, that is, to suffer for the

---

[18]   G. W. Lampe, *Reconciliation in Christ* (London: Longmans, Green and Company, 1955), pp. 60−61.

[19]   Brunner, *Dogmatics, II*, 182.

[20]   *Ibid.*, p. 183.

cause that Jesus suffered for us, our suffering is meaningful and receives the enduring strength, which springs from our fellowship with the suffering God. It is certainly true that "man can go through the most terrible sufferings if he sees a meaning in them; human powers of endurance are enormous,"[21] if he is related to God. Thus, "suffering that has meaning is bearable."[22]

Secondly, the fellowship of divine and human suffering maintains disciplined endurance to overcome our suffering in divine suffering. It seems to be the testimony of Paul's own experience that "suffering produces endurance" (Romans 5 : 3). However, suffering in itself does not necessarily strengthen our character to endure the infirmities of this world. Suffering gains enduring strength when it is related to a positive meaning, which is accompanied by the fellowship of divine and human suffering. As we have already stated, suffering is an enduring strength of *Agape,* and *Agape* without an element of suffering is a mere sentiment. If we believe that God is essentially *Agape* and our fellow-suffering with Him is also related to His essential nature, God's love becomes the source of our strength to overcome our suffering. The work of our own strength to overcome our suffering is transformed by the work of divine grace because our fellow-suffering with the divine is based on a sheer act of faith. It is, therefore, the power of divine grace, which is the source of our strength to overcome our suffering in divine suffering. In this respect, we can say with Paul, "It is no longer we who suffer, but God suffers in us." As our suffering becomes a part of God's eternal plan of salvation in the fellowship of divine and human fellowship, it is no longer we but God who becomes the subject of our suffering. This is perhaps what Bultmann may mean when he says:

... In this way, however, abandoning all illusions of selfmastery, he is to recognize himself before God as the man who exists purely and simply in dependence on God's grace. And in this very way he is pleasing to God, ans so he is open to receive the grace of God, whose "strength is made perfect in weakness": for—as Paul says—"When I am weak, then am I strong" (II Corinthians 12 : 9f). Out of suffering there develops for a man an inner strength in which he is superior to every trick of fate: suffering to him is a source of strength.[23]

Finally, the fellowship of divine and human suffering sustains in us the hope of anticipation, that is, the coming of the joy of eternal glory. The full anticipation of this joy is so great that "the sufferings of this present time are not

[21] Nicolas Berdyaev, *The Destiny of Man* (New York: Harper and Brothers, 1960), p. 119.

[22] Wayne E. Oates, *The Revelation of God in Human Suffering* (Philadelphia: The Westminster Press, 1959), p. 135.

[23] Rudolf Bultmann, Essays, *Philosophical and Theological,* trans. by J. C. Creig (London: S. C. M. Press, 1955), pp. 230–231.

worth comparing with the glory that is to be revealed to us" (Romans 8 : 18). Even though our temporal suffering is so oppressive and grievous, the joy of eternal glory, which is yet to come, still outweighs the temporal suffering (II Corinthians 4 : 17). This hope of glory does not disappoint us, because it is not something independent of, or apart from, the present experience of suffering. As the hope of tomorrow is latent in the faith of today,[24] the joy of eternal glory is also latent in the present moment of our fellow-suffering with God. The joy of "not yet" is implicit in that of "now already" (John 5 : 25). This is perhaps why Paul testifies, "We rejoice in our sufferings" (Romans 5 : 3). It is a paradox of Christian experience that any worthy experience of joy is latent in the experience of vicarious suffering. This idea is well illustrated by Hinton, who uses this paradox to attribute a concept of passibility of God.

. . . For if in the only worthy joy (the only happiness which matching the dignity of man or filling his capacity, rightly deserves the name of human), if in this there is necessarily latent the element of pain, so that by an absence it must be felt; —if in human joy is absorbed and taken up, not merely excluded or set aside, then we at once rise in our thoughts above ourselves. If this is our joy, then it is His also in whose image we were made. The pain that is latent in man's bliss is latent, too, in God's; in His most as He is highest and that great life and death to which the eyes of man are ever turned, or wandering ever are recalled, revealed it to us.[25]

This paradox of joy in suffering is closely related to Berdyaev's socalled "psychological paradox," in which "man may intensify his suffering in order that he may suffer less."[26] To apply this idea in our experience of joy in our fellow-suffering with God, we may get a psychological impression that our suffering is less than the actual suffering itself. Consequently, when we bear the yoke of suffering with Christ, the yoke is easy and burden is light (Matthew 11 : 30). In the fellowship of divine and human suffering, "the one and same burden is heavy and yet light,"[27] because of the joy of eternal glory which is both latent and anticipant in our experience of suffering with God. This hope of eternal glory that is promised in the suffering Christ eventually leads us to a *novum ultimum,* a renewal of all things.[28] It is then the re-

---

[24]   Brunner illustrates the relationship between faith and hope as follows: "As an expectant mother carried within her the child that is to be born, and awaits with certainty the event of its birth, so faith carries the future within it." See Brunner, *Dogmatics, III,* 342.

[25]   James Hinton, *The Mystery of Pain,* edited by James R. Nichols (Boston: Cupples, Upham and Company, 1886), pp. 50—51. The meaning of pain is to be understood as that of suffering.

[26]   Nicolas Berdyaev, *The Divine and the Human* (London: Geoffrey Bless, 1949), p. 76.

[27]   Søren Kierkegaard, *The Gospel of Suffering and the Lilies of the Field,* trans. by David F. Swenson and L. M. Swenson (Minneapolis: Augsburg Publishing House, 1948), p. 25.

[28]   Jürgen Moltmann, *Theology of Hope* (London: S. C. M., 1967), p. 33.

surrection hope which overcomes the suffering of the Cross. "Hope finds in Christ not only a consolation *in* suffering, but also the protest of the divine promise *against* suffering."[29] This hope sustains the meaning of suffering and "makes us ready to bear the 'Cross of the present.'"[30]

To sum up, our suffering can be overcome only in the fellowship of divine and human suffering, which sustains in us an ability to see the positive significance in our suffering, strength to endure the present moment of suffering, and the hope of anticipation in the joy of eternal glory. Thus, "within the fellowship of Christ's suffering, suffering is overcome by suffering."[31]

The last matter which we should like to examine is the fruit of being overcome in our suffering through the fellowship of divine and human suffering. The fruit of our endurance corresponds directly to the hope of anticipation, which is our participation in the joy of eternal glory. The actualization of this hope in our experience is, then, the fruit of being overcome in our suffering. It is the conviction of Paul that, if we suffer with God, we may also be glorified with Him (Romans 8 : 17). The realization of this glory of God in our experience is the reward of the present trial (I Peter 1 : 17,5 : 10). As the Resurrection is an answer to death, eternal glory is also the fruit of suffering. Moreover, because Jesus was crowned with glory and honor on account of His suffering and death (Hebrews 2 : 9), our union in His suffering may also lead to likeness in His glory. Therefore, the fruit of our endurance implies our empathic participation in the eternal glory, which has been imparted to us through the victory of Jesus Christ over the power of evil.

If the fruit of our endurance is to participate in the glory of God, what do we mean to participate in it? The Greek word *"doxa"* in the New Testament is the translation of the Hebrew word *"kabod,"* which originally denotes "weight" and came to be used significantly "in the sense of the visible brightness of the divine presence."[32] The glory is the illuminating presence of God Himself or the substance of divine presence. It uniquely belongs to God Himself, and, therefore, "all other glory (especially all the glory of men) can only copy Him."[33] Our participation in the glory of God, then, means the reflection of God's glory, which was originally the natural endowment of man before the Fall (Psalms 8 : 5). In other words, to participate in the glory of God is to be restored in the image of God, which was once lost but is now coming again from Christ, who is true image of God. Thus, the fruit of our

---

[29] *Ibid.,* p. 21.
[30] *Ibid.,* p. 31.
[31] Bonhoeffer, *The Cost of Discipleship,* p. 81.
[32] Cyril C. Richardson, *The Doctrine of the Trinity* (New York: The Abingdon Press, 1958), pp. 64–65.
[33] Barth, *Church Dogmatics, II/1,* 642.

endurence corresponds to the restoration of the divine image in us, which means our redemption.

If the participation in the glory of God means our redemption, our endurance is a means by which divine suffering redeems us through the Cross. That is, "suffering is necessary as a means to redemption, light and salvation."[34] The Cross of Christ, which is an all participating symbol of perfect endurance, is "the deepest and best means to the highest possible end,"[35] that is, the redemption of all mankind. Thus, the fruit of our endurance in our suffering with God is nothing other than our redemption through the Cross.

To be in the state of redemption does not mean to be free from the element of suffering. As long as there is evil in the world and sin in us, our suffering may continue within the fellowship of divine and human suffering. Nevertheless, when we are in the state of being redeemed, our suffering is lifted to a new level. Our "worldly grief" which produces death is changed to the "godly grief" which leads to salvation (II Corinthians 7 : 9–11). To be in the state of redemption is to separate from the existential estrangement, which is the basis of our evil suffering, to the essential union, which is that of our redemptive suffering with God. Thus, the existential meaning of the state of being redeemed does not imply the diminishing intensity of suffering on our part but the transitional value of suffering, that is, the transformation of the negative into the positive significance of suffering. As we have already pointed out, this transition is accompanied by the joy of sharing the eternal plan of salvation. This joy is not something without suffering but is in suffering with God. This joy in our endurance can be compared with the joy of the sculptor who wrestles with the recalcitrant block of marble or with that of the poet who struggles to bring an inadequate and clumsy vocabulary into the service of his vision.[36] It is the joy of bringing ourselves from all our ugliness and sin into the children of beauty and love who may become faithful disciples of Christ. One of the distinctive marks which comes from our endurance in our suffering with God is learning to obey. "Although he was a Son, he learned obedience through what he suffered" (Hebrews 5 : 8). "Without suffering one cannot learn obedience, for suffering is exactly the assurance that the devotion is not wilfulness; but he who learns obedience learns everything."[37] Through our endurance in suffering we come to learn that we are limited and we cannot control our own destiny. We learn from suffering that it is not we but God who rules the world. When we learn

---

[34] Berdyaev, *The Destiny of Man*, p. 120.

[35] Nels F. S. Ferré, *Evil and the Christian Faith* (New York: Harper and Brothers, 1947), p. 75.

[36] Robinson, *Suffering, Human and Divine*, pp. 195–196.

[37] Kierkegaard, *op. cit.*, pp. 212–213.

obedience from what we have suffered, our false pride which alienates us from God is transformed into real humility through humiliation. Furthermore, through endurance in our suffering with God we can enter into larger empathy with others. Genuine empathy with the suffering of other requires some experience of suffering, even though it may not be a similar experience. "For because he himself has suffered and been tempted, he is able to help those who are tempted" (Hebrews 2 : 18). From what we have suffered with God, we can learn not only to enlarge our sensitivity to share with and participate in the sorrow of others, but to deepen our assurance of God's love to forgive and to accept those who suffer in sin and evil. As Robinson says,

Suffering has opened the door into an avenue of life where may be won that prize of learning love which it is the great purpose of "life, with all it yields of joy and woe, and hope and fear" to offer us the chance of winning."[38]

Through our endurance in our suffering with God we are able to learn total obedience, real humility, genuine empathy and self-giving love. These are essential ingredients for the spiritual growth of human personality. Thus Kierkegaard believes that "only suffering trains for eternity."[39]

Nevertheless, the ultimate goal of our endurance in the fellowship of divine and human suffering is essentially an eschatological reality. The fruit of our endurance which we experience in the present time is only partial and analogous to the essential reality of redemption at the end of the world. Now we know and experience the fruit of victory in part, but, when the *telos* comes, we shall understand and experience it fully (I Corinthians 13 : 12). The hope of eternal glory, which is to be fully revealed to us, is anticipated with "a cosmic redemption – God's whole creation, despoiled by sin and death, will be set free" (Romans 8 : 18–20).[40] No one knows the day and hour of the end (Matthew 24 : 36) but the end will come with the most intense suffering that has ever been known since the creation of the world (Matthew 24 : 21). "When suffering is diffused, the end will come. This is the criterion for the arrival of the end."[41] Thus, the ultimate redemption will come with the diffusion of the most intense suffering, which is to be finally overcome with the *parousia*. Then, the hope of eternal glory becomes no longer the hope of anticipation but the present reality. The power of evil is eternally and completely swallowed up in the victory and blessedness where there is no more suffering, strife and pain in eternity. God will wipe away every tear from our eyes, "and death shall be no more, neither

[38]   Robinson, *op. cit.,* pp. 212–213.
[39]   Kierkegaard, *op. cit.,* p. 64.
[40]   John Knox, "The Epistle to the Romans: Introduction and Exegesis," *The Interpreter's Bible,* Vol. IX, edited by George Arthur Buttrick (New York: The Abingdon Press, 1954), p. 521.
[41]   Kazoh Kitamori, *Theology of the Pain of God* (Richmond: John Knox Press, 1965), p. 141.

shall there be mourning nor crying nor pain any more, for the former things have passed away" (Revelation 21 : 4).

To sum up, the fruit of overcoming our suffering in divine suffering is the actualization of our hope of anticipation, which is to partipate in the joy of eternal glory. To participate in the glory of God is to be restored in the image of God, which means our redemption. To be redeemed is to separate from the suffering of our existential estrangement, in order to reunite the separated with the redemptive suffering of God. Overcoming our suffering in divine suffering is existentially indispensable to the spiritual growth of our personality. However, the ultimate goal of our fellow-suffering with God is an eschatological reality. When the power of evil is ultimately overcome, our fellowship with God is essentially blessedness and peace. When we are ultimately redeemed, we are empathically united together in the community of eternal bliss, where the "I" participates no longer in the "Thou" of redemptive suffering but the "Thou" of eternal joy and peace. This is the ultimate goal of the world, which is promised through "the 'raising of the dead,' and the triumph of the resurrection life over death to the glory of the all-embracing lordship of God."[42]

---

[42] Moltmann, *op. cit.,* p. 302.

A THEOLOGICAL METHOD: AN ANALOGY OF FAITH

In the approach to a systematic inquiry into a concept of divine passibility, an analogy of faith (or an analogy of relation) is used as a theological method of interpretation. A question which immediately comes to mind is: "What is the criterion for choosing this method of investigation?" In order to respond to this question, in this Appendix it is intended: First, to justify the soundness of this method on biblical grounds. Secondly, the application and development of this method in the theology of Karl Barth is to be considered. Finally, the significance of this method for the approach to the problem of divine passibility is carefully examined.

Biblical Justification for an Analogy of Faith

An analogy is not the most satisfactory answer to the problem of theological epistemology. Neither the anthropomorphic way of thinking, which is deeply rooted in the very nature of man, nor the lofty idea of holiness, which is the very nature of divine, can be fully satisfied with an analogy. Nevertheless, the analogy is the inevitable choice of theological epistemology. If we believe that God is totally transcendent only, there is no way for us to know God. What we attempt to say about God then becomes purely an equivocal statement. On the other hand, if we believe that God is totally immanent only, there is no need for analogy in order to know God. Every statement which we make about God then becomes purely an anthropomorphic or a univocal statement. However, the God to whom the Old and New Testaments witness is *neither* the God of transcendence only *nor* the God of immanence only. He is neither partially transcendent nor partially immanent but is *both* totally transcendent *and* totally immanent at the same time. The paradoxical notion of this God, who is both transcendent and immanent at the same time, is the Hebraic and Christian concept of God.

The people of Israel were very sensitive to the transcendent nature of God, who dwells not on earth but in the heavenly place (I Kings 8 : 27; Psalms 123 : 1; Isaiah 33 : 5; II Kings 19 : 15, and others). At the same time the Psalmist describes the immanence of God, who not only searches the heart of man (Psalms 139 : 1–2) but never leaves him free from His presence (Psalms 139 : 7–8). Isaiah conceives of both the loftiness of divine transcendence (Isaiah 6 : 1) and the presence of divine immanence in Immanuel (Isaiah 7 : 14), who becomes the historical reality in the Incarnation of God in Jesus Christ (John 1 : 1–18; Philippians 2 : 6–8). In the Incarnation of God in Christ the paradoxical identity between transcendence and immanence becomes a divine mystery, in which man ceases to insist upon the validity of his own reasoning alone. This paradoxical identity between transcendence and immanence results in the inescapable tension between univocity and equivocity in our theological thinking. The outcome of this tension between univocity and equivocity is to be understood as an analogy, which is "a partial correspondence and agreement."[1] Whenever the paradoxical nature of God is expressed in terms of human language, the tension between univocity and equivocity accompanies it. Therefore the analogy, which is the by-product of this tension, is in a real sense not a human invention but a divine gift for our discernment of divine nature. In this respect, John McIntyre rightly expresses this view that the analogy is a God-given instrument for man: "Analogy is woven into the texture of Proclamation, and its presence there is not due to our inventiveness, but to God's will that it should be so."[2] In Romans 12 : 6 Paul calls this analogy the "analogy of faith" (ἀναλογία τῆς πίστεως).

The analogy of faith is translated in the Revised Standard Version as "proportion to our faith," because Paul has recognized that the analogous knowledge of God is given to him only through the faith in Christ. In other words, our understanding of God is relative to our faith. Isaiah illustrates it very simply when he says, "If you will not believe, you shall not understand" *(Nisi credideritis, non intelligetis).*[3] Consequently, the analogy of faith in Paul's thinking is quite similar to Anselm's concept of *"fides quaerens intellectum."*[4] According to the context in which Paul speaks of the analogy in Romans 12 : 6, "only the believers can exercise the χάρισμα; the power of the χάρισμα stands in   ἀναλογία   to the power of the faith appropriate to each."[5] The parallelism is also found in Romans 12 : 3, where Paul speake of God's

---

[1] Barth, *Church Dogmatics, III/1,* 225.
[2] John McIntyre, "Analogy," *The Scottish Journal of Theology,* Vol. XII (March, 1959), pp. 1–20.
[3] Quoted from the Old Latin versions of Isaiah 7 : 9; see also *Alan Richardson, An Introduction to the Theology of the New Testament* (New York: Harper and Brothers, 1958), p. 19.
[4] Karl Barth finds Paul's insight of the analogy of faith from his study of Anselm's *Fides Quaerens Intellectum,* where he has turned from dialectical to analogical thinking.
[5] Gerhard Kittel, "ἀναλογία," *Theological Dictionary of the New Testament,* Vol. I, ed. by Gerhard Kittel, Trans. by Geoffrey W. Bromiley (Grand Rapids: Wm. B. Eerdmans Publishing Company, 1964), p. 347.

dealing with us according to the measure of faith. In this verse, " μέτρος πίστεως" seems to imply "ἀναλογία τῆς πίστεως." Since our knowledge of God is in μέτρος or ἀναλογία to our πίστις, Paul recognizes our knowledge is imperfect as our faith is (I Corinthians 13 : 9). Paul refines this idea through the use of the analogy of the mirror. "For now we see in a mirror dimly, but then face to face. Now I know in part; then I shall understand fully, even as I have been fully understood" (I Corinthians 13 : 12). In this verse Paul introduces a new insight into the understanding of the nature of the analogy of faith. According to this, the analogy is indirect knowledge, that is, a reflection or a copy of real knowledge. Therefore, our understanding of God in proportion to our faith is not real knowledge but only a copy of it.

Paul's concept of the "ἀναλογία τῆς πίστεως" gives another important clue to the understanding of its real meaning. He uses the definite article "τῆς" for faith. It seems reasonable to think that Paul consciously distinguishes "faith" from "the faith." In his thought "faith" may be said to have come before the law was given (Galatians 3 : 6–9, 15–18; Romans 4), but "the faith" is faith in Jesus Christ which came after the law (Galatians 3 : 23, 25). It was only after the events of Easter and pentecost that "faith" became "the faith," that is, the faith in Jesus Christ whom God made the Lord and Christ (Acts 2 : 36).[6]

Characteristically the Johannine use of πιστεύειν followed by εἰς is similar to the Pauline use of the faith, which "is not the regular *fidei* of the objective content of Christian faith or the doctrine of faith *(quae creditur),*"[7] but implies the personal character of faith in Jesus Christ. This personal character of faith implies a trustful relationship with a person (e.g., πιστεύετε εἰς τὸν θεόν, χαὶ εἰς ἐμὲ πιστεύετε, John 14 : 1).[8] Therefore, the ἀναλογία τῆς πίστεως is always characterized in terms of a relationship within a personal category. This personal relationship, which is a characteristic of this analogy, is certainly central to the dynamic aspect of the Christian faith. Consequently, this analogy is an analogy of relations, which is distinguished from an analogy of being.

Since the analogy of faith, which characterizes a personal correspondence, is based on faith in Jesus Christ, our faith in God is possible only through the faith in a corresponding being, the being of God-man, in whom we are related to God. In the New Testament, it is closely related with γινώσκειν.[9]

[6] Cyril C. Richardson, *The Doctrine of the Trinity* (New York: The Abingdon Press, 1958), p. 24.

[7] Kittel, *op. cit.,* p. 347.

[8] "The peculiarly Johannine πιστεύειν εἰς τὸ ὄνομα (1 : 12; 2 : 23; 3 : 18) is probably a reference to the baptismal confession of faith in Christ's name." See Richardson, *op. cit.,* p. 45.

[9] For example, Peter confesses that "We have believed, and have come to know, that you are the Holy One of God" (John 6 : 69).

To have our faith in Christ is the acting by which we come to know Him. Knowing results in believing, while the latter is conditioned by the former. Therefore, γινώσκειν generally in the New Testament and especially in Johannine usage means to enter into relations with someone through πιστεύειν. Then, knowing is always "seeing with the eye of faith; and this is a position which is fully biblical and in the common teaching of the New Testament."[10] It is Philip who has appealed to Jesus "Lord, show us the Father" (John 14 : 8). Then, Jesus replies: "He who has seen me has seen the Father" (John 14 : 9). It is the distinctively Johannine emphasis that to know Christ is to know God, because Jesus came from the Father (John 8 : 23) in order to reveal Him and make Him known among men (John 1 : 18). Jesus is the only way which leads to the Father (John 14 : 6), and He is in the Father and the Father in Him (John 14 : 10, 11). This idea is not alien to the Synoptic writers, who also believe that there is no true knowledge of God apart from the revelation of God in Christ. "All things have been delivered to me by my Father; and no one knows the Son except the Father, and no one knows the Father except the Son and anyone to whom the Son chooses to reveal Him" (Matthew 11 : 27; Luke 10 : 22). Therefore, our knowledge of God, which is always analogous, is possible only in our loving relation to Jesus Christ who is the source and foundation of the analogy of faith. In other words, the distinctive mark of this analogy is its Christological approach. This is the conviction of Paul when he says, "From now on, therefore, we regard no one from a human point of view; even though we once regarded Christ from a human point of view, we regard him thus no longer" (II Corinthians 5 : 16). It is "the Spirit searches everything, even the depths of God" (I Corinthians 2 : 10).

To sum up, it is the biblical concept of God, whose paradoxical identity between transcendence and immanence, which presses us to make an inevitable choice of the word "analogy," which stands somewhat between "univoca" and "aequivoca."[11] The analogy which the New Testament and especially Paul speak of is the analogy of faith, which implies the cognitive significance of faith in Christ. It is characterized by dynamic, personal and christological categories.

The Application and Development of the Analogy of Faith in the Theology of Karl Barth

The Pauline concept of the analogy of faith has been applied and developed

[10] Richardson, *op. cit.*, p. 47.

[11] The "univoca" means "the same term, applied to two different objects in the same way, designates the same thing in both of them." The "aequivoca" means "the same term, applied to two different objects, designates different things in the one and the other." See Barth, *Church Dogmatics, II/1,* 237.

as an alternative to the analogy of being in the theology of Karl Barth. Barth is perhaps the first Protestant theologian who uses the analogy of faith over against the Roman Catholic Church.[12] Moreover, Pehlmann believes that Barth's use of the analogy of faith is a theological new-creation (Die analogia fidei Barths ist eine theologische Neuschöpfung).[13] The development of this new insight in Barth's theology can be conceived in terms of a slow evolution from his dialectical thinking. There have been two radical turning points in the development of his theological thinking; the first is in the publication of his Römerbrief, where he turned from liberal to dialectical thinking through the reinterpretation of Kierkegaard's concept of the infinite qualitative distinction between time and eternity; and the second is in his study of Anselm's *Fides Quaerens Intellectum,* where he turned from dialectical to analogical thinking. Within his *Church Dogmatics* there is also a progressive evolvement of his analogical thinking. Since the publication of *Church Dogmatics III/1* in 1945, he is no longer engaged in polemic against the Roman Catholic doctrine of *analogia entis.*

In the understanding of Barth's analogical thinking, it is rather useful first to consider his negative reaction to an analogy of being. His rejection of the analogy of being as "the invention of anti-Christ"[14] is in fact that it becomes the core of natural theology. Therefore, the analogy of being is unable to conceive God as the Lord, Creator, Reconciler and Redeemer.[15] Since the analogy of being is the inner core of natural theology, Barth regards the repudiation of the latter as that of the former.

Several assumptions which underlie Barth's theology for the rejection of the analogy of being as the root of natural theology can be briefly summerized as follows: In the first place, Barth assumes that there is no other avenue of knowing God than through the revelation of God in Jesus Christ. Thus, the analogy of being, which seeks God apart from the revelation of God in Christ, is a wasteful and worthless attempt. In the second place, he assumes that the task of theology is primarily the task of expounding a knowledge about God drawn from the Holy Scripture. Therefore, the analogy of being, which is not based on the main line of biblical thinking,[16] introduces an alien task which is quite contrary to the real task of expounding the Scripture. Finally, Barth assumes that there is an infinite qualitative distinction between God and

---

[12] Brunner, *Dogmatics, II,* 42.
[13] Horst Georg Pehlmann, *Analogia entis oder Analogia fidei: Die Frage der Analogie bei Karl Barth* (Goettingen: Vandenhoeck und Ruprecht, 1965), p. 112.
[14] Barth, *Church Dogmatics, I/1,* x.
[15] Barth, *Church Dogmatics, II/1,* 75–79.
[16] *Ibid.,* pp. 102, 113; Psalms 8 and 104 which are frequently quoted for the justification of natural theology are not recognized as the "main line" of biblical thought.

man, that is not longer real in Jesus Christ.[17] Thus, the God who reveals Himself in Christ is totally different from the God who is in the sphere of man's cognition.[18]

To sum up, the fundamental motives which led Barth to repudiate the concept of the analogy of being may be stated as follows: (1) The analogy of being reduces the qualitative distinction between God and man to the quantitative distinction between them. Thus, it seeks God within the category of human reason. (2) Consequently, the analogy of being assumes that God is directly accessible to us apart from the revelation of God in Jesus Christ. Thus, it believes that knowledge of God is possible in natural man prior to and apart from God's encounter in Christ. (3) The analogy of being is an attempt of man to find God, rather than God's coming to seek man. Thus, it is a counterpole to the Grace which moves downward. (4) Finally, the analogy of being "makes out of the 'He' an 'it,' out of becoming a being."[19] Thus, a God who is static and impersonal is quite contrary to our God, who is always dynamic and personal in His relation to us.

Barth's repudiation of the concept of the analogy of being does not imply that there is no possibility for the use of analogy in his theological thinking. To deny the use of analogy is in fact to escape the necessity of considering the relation of man with God altogether.[20] Barth recognizes the necessity of a means to receive the Word of God. "For if we know Him," Barth said, "we know Him by means given us, otherwise we do not know Him at all."[21] The means which is given to us by the Grace of God cannot be either parity or disparity but must be analogy. Since this analogy is the gift of God, it must be accepted in faith alone. Therefore, it is not the analogy of being but the analogy of faith. This is why Barth claims that "there is no '*analogia entis*,'" but "there is only an '*analogia fidei*.'"[22] However, the term "*analogia relationis*" is often used to signify the analogy of faith. There is no real distinction between them, even though an arbitrary differentiation can be made in terms of their emphasis and the context in which they are used. The term "*analogia fidei*" is used to imply primarily the epistemological function of analogy and to deal with the context in which an epistemological question is raised.[23] On the other hand, the term "*analogia relationis*" is used to deal primarily with the ontological aspect of analogy and in the context of ontic relation,

[17]   Karl Barth, *The Humanity of God* (Richmond: John Knox Press, 1960), p. 36ff.
[18]   Barth, *Church Dogmatics*, II/1, 86.
[19]   *Ibid.*, p. 231.
[20]   E. L. Mascall, *Existence and Analogy: A Sequel to "He Who Is"* (London: Longmans, Green and Company, 1959), p. 92.
[21]   Barth, *Church Dogmatics*, II/1, 225.
[22]   Barth, *Church Dogmatics*, I/1, 501.
[23]   See especially in Barth's *Church Dogmatics*, II/1.

that is, God's relation to the image of God and creation.[24] However, both the analogy of faith and the analogy of relation are synonymously used in his theology as a whole.

The analogy of faith means "the correspondence (in faith) of the thing known with the knowing, of the object with the thought, of the Word of God with the word of man in thought and in speech."[25] In other words, it is the correspondence and similarity in faith, in spite of all dissimilarity of the relationship between God and man. The correspondence and similarity between God and man can take place only in faith, because faith is "an act of human decision corresponding to the act of divine decision."[26] In this faith it is not man but God who has effected and is effecting the communication of Himself to man. Since the analogy of faith is created and given to us through the gracious revelation of God in Christ,[27] God in Christ becomes its *analogans* and man its *analogatum.*[28] On the other hand, since the analogy of being is created by the being of the world, man becomes the *analogans* and God the *analogatum.* Thus, the conflict between the analogy of faith and that of being can be made in terms of the conflict of movement between the *analogans* and *analogatum.*

This movement of the *analogans* to the *analogatum* is a key to understanding the epistemological function of analogy. In the analogy of faith God always becomes the *analogans* and man the *analogatum,* because man cannot know God unless God gives Himself to be known in the revelation of His word through the Holy Spirit. In other words, the revelation of God cannot be inferred from the general concept of human cognition and language.[29] Therefore, "in His revelation God lowers Himself to be known by us according to the measure of our own human cognition."[30] Our thinking and language may be similar to empty shells which God fills with His own word. In this way God as He who is inHimself and as He who is known is not the other but the same God. For example, the words "father" and "son" do not first have their truth in our thought and language but their origins are in God's revelation.[31] Therefore, "whatever is said by ours was, is and will be said truly in Him."[32] Especially in our preaching and sacraments, our language is sanctified and

---

[24]   See especially in Barth's *Church Dogmatics, III/1.*
[25]   Barth, *Church Dogmatics, I/1,* 279.
[26]   Barth, *Church Dogmatics, II/1,* 26.
[27]   *Ibid.,* p. 85.
[28]   Barth, *Church Dogmatics, IV/3,* 770.
[29]   Barth, *Church Dogmatics, I/1,* 158.
[30]   Barth, *Church Dogmatics, II/1,* 61.
[31]   *Ibid.,* p. 229.
[32]   *Ibid.,* p. 228.

transformed into the language about God through the work of the Holy Spirit.[33] To sum up, the epistemological function of the analogy of faith is due to "a contradiction between form and content."[34] The form of analogy, which is the mode of signification, is human, and the content of it is God Himself. The divine content (or the *analogans)* takes unto itself the human form (or the *analogatum),* but the latter is inadequate to express the former. Consequently, our knowledge of God is a partial correspondence.

While the epistemological function of the analogy of faith is oriented in polemic against the analogy of being, the ontological aspect of it is positive in the approach to Barth's theological method. In the doctrine of the image of God, Barth recognizes that the importance of this analogy is to provide a framework in which the relationship between man and God is realized. Even though Barth once insisted the total annihilation of the image of God in the fall,[35] he now restates that through the analogy of relation the image of God is none other than the true *humanum* in confrontation with his followers, especially with woman. In other words, man is of the image of God, not because of a special quality of being possessed by God, but because it signifies the universal constituent of man's humanity.[36] His affirmation of the image of God is possible only in that he can conceive it as a copy of the true image, that is, Jesus Christ Himself. Man's image of God is, then, nothing other than the reflection or copy of that true image which is revealed in Jesus Christ. Therefore, the analogy of relation has provided the basic framework in which not only the new and positive apprehension of the image of God, man's humanity in encounter with woman, is realized but also his growing appreciation of the concept of "I-Thou" encounter.

The concept of I-Thou relationship can be understood by Barth in terms of the analogy of relation. The analogy of relation between God and man is "simply the existence of the I and the Thou in confrontation."[37] Barth believes that this I-Thou relationship must first exist in Godhead, and then confront the man whom He has created. In other words, the human I-Thou relation is due to the divine I-Thou relationship. The characteristic nature of God is that He has the I-Thou inHimself, while the characteristic nature of man's I-Thou relationship is that he is man and woman (the husband and wife relationship). This I-Thou relation in Godhead is the prototype of that rela-

---

[33] Barth, *Church Dogmatics, I/1,* 53–54.
[34] *Ibid.,* p. 466ff.
[35] *Ibid.,* p. 273.
[36] Barth, *Church Dogmatics, III/1,* 186: "He would not be man if he were not the image of God. He is the iamge of God in fact that he is man."
[37] Barth, *Church Dogmatics, IV/1,* 185.

tion in man.[38] In spite of the similarity and correspondence between human and divine encounter, the divine I-Thou is quite different from the human I-Thou. The I-Thou relationship in the Godhead takes place in the one and unique individual, while the I-Thou in humanity takes place in two different individuals, the man and woman.[39] Moreover, because the human I-Thou is the copy of the divine I-Thou, the former is quite distinct from the latter. Therefore, the function of the analogy, which is not to relate the similar but the dissimilar relations,[40] is to relate these two dissimilar I-Thou relationships. The correspondence and the similarity between these two relationships are possible only because of a corresponding being, the being of God-man in Jesus Christ, who relates both in Himself. Therefore, Christology is the essence of the analogy of relation.

To sum up, the basic principle by which Barth operates his analogical thinking is in "act," rather than in "being." This does not mean that "being" is completely ignored. A being becomes actual in that it is active, and the act presupposes the being. Consequently, everything, even God, man and the world, must be conceived in terms of this dynamic, living and personal relationship through the corresponding being, the being of God-man in Christ. Pehlmann calls this kind of relationship which involves everything as *"Panaktualismus,"*[41] which can be compared with an hour-glass in which the sands come down from above through the narrow place in the middle. Here, God is depicted as an "Act," that is, God's coming to the world through the "narrow middle," which represents Jesus Christ. God is not really God in Himself without the "Act," while the "Act" is possible only in Jesus Christ. At the same time, man is no longer a man in himself but only in active relation to woman in Christ. Moreover, the world is not a real world in itself but only in its relation to Christ. Thus, everything including God, man and the world is active *in* and *through* the corresponding being, the being of God-man in Jesus Christ. Barth's analogical thinking is then simply summed up as the similarity and correspondence of a dynamic and personal relationship between God and man in and through Jesus Christ. It seems quite clear that his struggle against the analogy of being is fundamentally his struggle against the concept of the static and impersonal relationship which is based on a speculative theory of a hierarchy of being and is not the biblical idea. In conclusion, the application and development of the analogy of faith in Barth's

---

[38]   Barth, *Church Dogmatics, III/2,* 218: "He is the original and source of every I and Thou, of the I which is eternally from and to the Thou and therefore supremely I."

[39]   Barth, *Church Dogmatics, III/1,* 196.

[40]   *Ibid.:* "Analogy, even as the analogy of relation, does not entail likeness but the correspondence of the unlike."

[41]   Pehlmann, *op. cit.,* p. 117.

theology signifies the triumph of faith-knowledge over human reason to know God.

The Significance of the Analogy of Faith for the Problem of Divine Passibility

Why is the analogy of faith a theological method for the problem of divine passibility? Is this method the most adequate to deal with the problem? As has already been suggested in the beginning of this chapter, the analogy is an inevitable choice of theological term to describe the divine mystery. God, who is both transcendent and immanent at the same time, cannot be conceived in terms of either anthropomorphism (or univocity) or theomorphism (or equivocity) but analogy. Anthropomorphism tends to make God identical with man, while theomorphism tends to eliminate from God every human association. Thus, the analogy is the only possible way of finite creature to express the paradoxical tension between anthropomorphism and theomorphism. If every thing that we say, think and feel about divine nature is an analogous statement, our approach to the problem of divine passibility ought to be analogical. Then, why is not the analogy of being but the analogy of faith a theological method to be applied here? In order to answer this question we may examine the compatibility of the analogy of faith with the concept of divine passibility.

To see the compatibility of the analogy of faith with the concept of divine passibility, we may briefly summarize the basic characteristics of this analogy in comparison with those of the analogy of being. According to Karl Barth, the characteristics of these analogies are quite contrary to each other. First of all, the analogy of faith signifies the cognitive significance of faith, while the analogy of being the cognitive significance of human reason. In other words, the former seeks God within the category of faith in Christ, while the latter within the category of human reason. Secondly, the analogy of faith presupposes the corresponding being, God-man, in Jesus Christ, while the analogy of being assumes that God is directly accessible to us without a corresponding being. Thus, the former is the Christological but the latter is a natural approach to the understanding of divine nature. Thridly, the analogy of faith deals with a personal relationship, while the analogy of being the impersonal relationship. It is not the former but the latter which makes God, who is always the Subject, the object of man through the use of a human category. Finally, the analogy of faith is dynamic, while the analogy of being static in nature. Therefore, the analogy of faith, which signifies God s coming to be known in faith, is characterized by the christological, personal and dynamic categories. On the other hand, the analogy of being, which signifies man's approach to know God in reason, is characterized by the natural, impersonal and static categories. Since the problem of divine possibility is the problem of divine pathos, which is an essential aspect of a personal and living God, the analogy of faith, which uses these categories, seems better equipped than the analogy of being in dealing with the problem. A closer examination of the compatibility of the analogy of faith with the problem of divine passibility may help us to realize the significance of this method for the purpose of our investigation.

In the first place, the concept of divine passibility ought not to be deduced from our human experience, because the divine pathos, which signifies the ontological aspect of divine passibility, is a mystery to us. As Heschel made clear, "What Isaiah (55 : 8f.) said concerning the thoughts of God may equally apply to His pathos: For my pathos is not your pathos, neither are your ways my ways, says the Lord."[42] With the finiteness and blindness of human emotion we cannot reason directly from our own experience the concept of divine pathos, which is not limited in time and space. As Brunner says, the concept of divine possibility represents the highest point of contrast with the abstract and speculative idea of God.[43] Thus, the concept of divine passibility cannot be comprehended by syllogism, analysis or induction, but only through divine participation in us, that is, the empathy of God. This divine participation becomes actual in our faith in Christ. It is, therefore, not the analogy of being, which seeks divine nature in human reason, but the analogy of faith, which seeks it in faith, capable of approaching the problem of divine passibility.

In the second place, the very nature of Christianity is a personal religion. As Calvin Linton says, "impersonal religion is contradiction in terms."[44] Thus, the analogy of being which subscribes the impersonal category of expression is irrelevant to the Christian concept of God, whose very nature is a personal Being. The analogy of faith, which implies the correspondence and similarity between two dissimilar personal relations, that is, between the I-Thou relationship in Godhead and the I-Thou relationship in humanity, is able to apprehend the pathos of God which is the very essence of a personal God. This I-Thou relationship is to be understood in terms of empathy. In other words, there is first a mutual participation in the Godhead; the participation of the Son in the Father and the Father in the Son through the Holy Spirit. And the mutual participation in Godhead reflects the empathic relation

---

[42]   Abraham J. Heschel, *The Prophets* (New York: Harper and Row, 1962), p. 276.
[43]   Brunner, *Dogmatics, I,* 274.
[44]   Calvin Linton, "The Depersonalization of God," *Christianity Today* (April 10, 1964), p. 12.

in humanity, that is, the participation of one another through love. It is a weakness of Barth's thinking to limit the I-Thou relationship in humanity to the relationship of man and woman only. It must be an inclusive personal relationship, which takes into account the empathic relationship in every dimension of life, such as the parent and child relation, the man and woman relation and the I-fellow relation. The task of the analogy of faith is to relate the prototype of empathic relation in God to every empathic relationship in humanity through a corresponding being, which is the perfect empathy of God in Christ.

In the third place, a key to the understanding of divine passibility is the corresponding being, the Being of God-man in Jesus Christ. Nevertheless, the analogy of being attempts to find the divine without this corresponding being. As Brasnett says, "There is always a risk in arguing directly from the human to the divine, for God's ways are not always our ways."[45] Kitamori regards this kind of direct approach to the divine, the divine love as the "immediate (im-mediate) love,"[46] love without mediator and without pain. It is certainly strange, shocking and quite opposed to what we naturally expect our God to be when God approaches us in Christ as the form of Suffering Servant. In this way God gives us this corresponding being, which Relton calls "the given."[47] "The given" is the basis of the analogy of faith. "For this reason," Barth believes, "theology can think and speak only as it looks at Jesus Christ and from the vantage point of what He is."[48] Consequently, the analogy of being, which eliminates "the given" or the corresponding being, is almost incapable of understanding divine passibility. On the other hand, the analogy of faith, which necessitates "the given" or the perfect empathy of God in Christ, is congenial to the understanding of divine passibility.

In the last place, the God of the Bible is not "like an immobile piece of stone,"[49] but is a living God who is filled with life and drama in history. The living God who participates in the suffering of the world is clear evidence that God is capable of sharing the suffering of others, because the feeling is an indispensable part of the living God. Nevertheless, the static God is not only incapable of feeling but He is *actus purus,* actuality without potentiality of anything more."[50] Thus, the analogy of being which subscribes the

---

[45] Bertrand R. Brasnett, *The Suffering of the Impassible God* (London: S. P. C. K., 1928), p. 117.

[46] Kazoh Kitamori, *Theology of the Pain of God* (Richmond: John Knox Press, 1965), p. 38.

[47] H. Maurice Relton, *Studies in Christian Doctrine* (London: The Macmillan Company, 1960), p. 1.

[48] Karl Barth, *The Humanity of God* (Richmond: John Knox Press, 1960), p. 55.

[49] O. Fielding Clarke, *God and Suffering* (London: Peter Smith, 1964), p. 44.

[50] Edgar S. Brightman, *The Problem of God* (New York: The Abingdon Press, 1930), p. 175.

static nature of God is incompatible with the concept of divine passibility. On the other hand, the analogy of faith, which is based on the dynamic ontology, is the most congenial method in the approach to the problem of divine passibility.

In conclusion, a theological method of our investigation to the problem of divine passibility is the analogy of faith. The congeniality of this analogy to accomodate the pathos of God is due to its dynamic, personal and Christological approaches.

BIBLIOGRAPHY

Allport, Gordon W. *Personality: A Psychological Interpretation*. New York: H. Holt and Company, 1937.

Anderson, Bernhard W. *Understanding the Old Testament*. Englewood Cliffs, New Jersey: Prentice-Hall, Inc., 1957.

Aristotle. *Ethica Nicomachea*. Edited by W. D. Ross. Oxford: The Clarendon Press, 1925.

Aristotle. "Metaphysics." *Philosophers Speak for Themselves; From Aristotle to Plotinus*. Edited by T. V. Smith. Chicago: University of Chicago Press, 1956.

Arnold, E. Vernon. *Roman Stoicism: Being Lectures on the History of the Stoic Philosophy with Special Reference to its Development within the Roman Empire*. New York: The Humanities Press, 1958.

Aulén, Gustaf. *Christus Victor: An Historical Study of the Idea of the Atonement*. London: S. P. C. K., 1931.

— . *The Faith of the Christian Church*. Trans. by Eric H. Wahlstrom and G. Everett Arden. Philadelphia: The Muhlenberg Press, 1948.

Ayer, Joseph Cullen. *A Source Book for Ancient Church History: From the Apostolic Age to the Close of the Conciliar Period*. New York: Charles Scribner's Sons, 1941.

Baillie, Donald M. *God Was in Christ*. New York: Charles Scribner's Sons, 1948.

Baillie, John. *The Place of Jesus Christ in Modern Christianity*. New York: Charles Scribner's Sons, 1929.

— . *Our Knowledge of God*. New York: Charles Scribner's Sons, 1939.

— . *The Idea of Revelation in Recent Thought*. New York: Columbia University Press, 1956.

Barth, Karl. *Church Dogmatics. The Doctrine of the Word of God*, Vol. I. *The Doctrine of God*, Vol. II. *The Doctrine of Creation*, Vol. III. *The Doctrine of Reconciliation*, Vol. IV. Trans. by G. W. Bromiley and T. F. Torrance. Edinburgh: T. and T. Clark, 1936–1961.

— . *The Knowledge of God and Service of God According to the Teaching of the Reformation*. London: Hodder and Stoughton, 1938.

— . *Dogmatics in Outline*. London: S. C. M. Press, 1949.

— . *The Humanity of God*. Richmond: John Knox Press, 1960.

— . *Credo*. New York: Charles Scribner's Sons, 1962.

Berdyaev, Nicolas. *The Divine and the Human*. London: Geoffrey Bless, 1949.

— . *The Destiny of Man*. New York: Harper and Brothers, 1960.

Berkhof, Hendrikus. *The Doctrine of the Holy Spirit: The Annie Kinkead Warfield Lectures, 1963–1964*. Richmond: John Knox Press, 1964.

Bertocci, Peter A. *An Introduction to the Philosophy of Religion*. Englewood Cliffs, New Jersey: Prentice-Hall, Inc., 1951.

Blackman, E. C. "Incarnation." *The Interpreter's Dictionary of the Bible, E-J.* New York: The Abingdon Press, 1962.

Bonhoeffer, Dietrich. *Prisoner for God: Letters and Papers from Prison.* Trans. by R. H. Fuller. New York: The Macmillan Company, 1954.

−. *Ethics.* Edited by Eberhard Bethge. Trans. by Neville H. Smith. London: S. C. M. Press, 1955.

−. *Temptation.* Edited by Eberhard Bethge. Trans. by Kathleen Downham. London: S. C. M. Press, 1955.

−. *The Cost of Discipleship.* Trans. by R. H. Fuller. New York: The Macmillan Company, 1959.

−. *Creation and Fall: A Theological Interpretation of Genesis 1−3.* Trans. by John C. Flecher. London: S. C. M. Press, 1959.

−. *The Communion of Saints: A Dogmatic Inquiry into the Sociology of the Church.* New York: Harper and Row, 1963.

Bouquet, A. C. *The Doctrine of God: Final Studies in the Divine Nature and Attributes, with Chapters on the Philosophy of Worship.* Cambridge: W. Heffer and Son, 1934.

Brasnett, Bertrand R. *The Suffering of the Impassible God.* London: S. P. C. K., 1928.

Brightman, Edgar S. *The Problem of God.* New York: The Abingdon Press, 1930.

−. *The Finding of God.* New York: The Abingdon Press, 1931.

−. *Is God a Person?* New York: Association Press, 1932.

−. *A Philosophy of Religion.* Englewood Cliffs, New Jersey: Prentice-Hall, Inc., 1940.

Broomall, Wick. *The Holy Spirit: A Scriptural Study of His Person and Work.* New York: American Tract Society, 1940.

Brown, Delwin, *et al.,* eds. *Process Philosophy and Christian Thought.* New York: Bobbs-Merrill, 1971.

Brunner, Emil. *The Christian Doctrine of God: Dogmatics, Vol. I.* Trans. by Olive Wyon. Philadelphia: The Westminster Press, 1950.

−. *The Christian Doctrine of Creation and Redemption: Dogmatics, Vol. II.* Trans. by Olive Wyon. Philadelphia: The Westminster Press, 1952.

−. *Faith, Hope and Love.* Philadelphia: The Westminster Press, 1956.

−. *The Christian Doctrine of the Church, Faith and the Consummation: Dogmatics, Vol. III.* Trans. by David Cairns in collaboration with T. H. L. Parker. Philadelphia: The Westminster Press, 1960.

Buckman, John W. *The Humanity of God: An Interpretation of the Divine Fatherhood.* New York: Harper and Brothers, 1928.

Bultmann, Rudolf. *Essays, Philosophical and Theological.* Trans. by J. C. Creig. London: S. C. M. Press, 1955.

−. *Jesus and the World.* Trans. by Louise P. Smith and Erminie H. Lantero. New York: Charles Scribner's Sons, 1958.

−. *Faith and Understanding,* I. Edited by R. W. Funk. Trans. by L. P. Smith. London: S. C. M. Press, 1969.

Burnley, Edward. "Impassibility of God." *The Expository Times,* Vol. 67, October, 1955 - September, 1956, pp. 90−91.

Clark, O. Fielding. *God and Suffering.* London: Peter Smith, 1964

Dentan, Robert C. *The King and His Cross.* New York: Seabury Press, 1965.

Dewick, E. C. *The Indwelling God: A Historical Study of the Christian Conception of Divine Immanence and Incarnation, with Special Reference to Indian Thought.* London: Oxford University Press, 1938.

Dillistone, F. W. *The Significance of the Cross.* Philadelphia: The Westminster Press, 1944.

—. *Jesus Christ and His Cross.* Philadelphia: The Westminster Press, 1952.

Dodd, C. H. *The Interpretation of the Fourth Gospel.* Cambridge: The University Press, 1960.

Fairbairn, Andrew M. *The Place of Christ in Modern Theology.* New York: Charles Scribner's Sons, 1893.

Ferré, Nels F. S. *Evil and the Christian Faith.* New York: Harper and Brothers, 1947.

—. *The Christian Understanding of God.* New York: Harper and Brothers, 1951.

—. *Reason in Religion.* London: Nelson, 1962.

Foreman, Kenneth Joseph. *Identification: Human and Divine.* Richmond: John Knox Press, 1963.

Forsyth, P. T. *The Person and Place of Jesus Christ.* London: Independent Press, 1909.

Franks, Robert. "Passibility and Impassibility." *Encyclopedia of Religion and Ethics,* IX. Edited by James Hastings. New York: Charles Scribner's Sons, 1924.

Galloway, Allan D. *The Cosmic Christ.* New York: Harper and Brothers, 1951.

Gibran, Kahlil. *The Prophet.* New York: Alfred A. Knopf, 1956.

Gollwitzer, Helmut, *et al.,* eds. *Dying We Live: The Final Messages and Records of Some Germans Who Defied Hitler.* Trans. by Reinhard C. Kuhn. London: The Harvill Press, 1956.

Grant, Frederick C. *An Introduction to New Testament Thought.* New York: The Abingdon Press, 1950.

Heschel, Abraham J. *The Prophets.* New York: Harper and Row, 1966.

Hick, John. *Evil and the God of Love.* New York: Harper and Row, 1966.

Hinton, James. *The Mystery of Pain.* Edited by James R. Nichols. Boston: Cupples, Upham, and Company, 1886.

Hippolytus. "Against the Heresy of One Noetus." *Ante-Nicene Fathers: Translations of the Writings of the Fathers Down to A.D. 325,* V. Edited by Alexander Roberts and James Donaldson. Grand Rapids: Wm. B. Eerdmans Publishing Company, 1957.

Holmes, John H. "A Struggling God." *My Idea of God: A Symposium of Faith.* Edited by Joseph Fort Newton. Boston: Little, Brown Company, 1926.

Hooker, Morna D. *Jesus and the Servant: The Influence of the Servant Concept of Deutero-Isaiah in the New Testament.* London: S. P. C. K., 1959.

Inge, William Ralph. *The Philosophy of Plotinus: The Gifford Lectures at St. Andrews, 1917–1918,* I. London: Longmans, Green and Company, 1929.

Jenkins, Daniel T. *The Christian Belief in God.* Philadelphia: The Westminster Press, 1964.

Johnson, Paul E. *Psychology of Pastoral Care.* New York: The Abindon Press, 1953.

Kierkegaard. Søren. *Concluding Unscientific Postscript.* Trans. by David F. Swenson. Princeton: Princeton University Press, 1941.

—. *The Gospel of Suffering and the Lilies of the Field.* Trans. by David F. Swenson and L. M. Swenson. Minneapolis: Augsburg Publishing House, 1948.

Kitamori, Kazoh. *Theology of the Pain of God.* Richmond: John Knox Press, 1965.

Kittel, Gerhard. "ἀναλογία," *Theological Dictionary of the New Testament,* I. Edited by Gerhard Kittel. Trans. by Geoffrey W. Bromiley. Grand Rapids: Wm. B. Eerdmans Publishing Company, 1964.

Knight, Harold. *The Hebrew Prophetic Consciousness.* London: Lutterworth Press, 1947.

Knox, John. "The Epistle to the Romans: Introduction and Exegesis." *The Interpreter's Bible*, IX. Edited by George Arthur Buttrick. New York: The Abingdon Press, 1954.

Knudson, Albert C. *The Doctrine of God*. New York: The Abingdon Press, 1930.

−. *Doctrine of Redemption*. New York: The Abingdon Press, 1933.

Lampe, G. W. *Reconciliation in Christ*. London: Longmans, Green and Company, 1955.

Lavelle, Louis. *Evil and Suffering*. Trans. by Bernard Murchland. New York: The Macmillan Company, 1963.

Lee, Jung Young. "Interpreting the Demonic Powers in Pauline Thought." *Novum Testamentum*, XII, Fase. 1, January, 1970, 54−69.

−. "Karl Barth's Use of Analogy in His Church Dogmatics." *The Scottish Journal of Theology*, XXII, No. 2 (June, 1969), 129−151.

−. "Bultmann's Existentialist Interpretation and the Problem of Evil." *Journal of Religious Thought*, XXVI, No. 3 (Autumn-Winter), 65−80.

−. "The Yin-Yang Way of Thinking: A Possible Method for Ecumenical Theory." *International Review of Mission*, LX, No. 239 (July, 1971), 363−370.

−. *The I: A Christian Concept of Man*. New York: Philosophical Library, 1971.

−. *The Principle of Changes: Understanding the I Ching*. New Hyde Park: University Books, 1971.

Linton, Calvin. "The Depersonalization of God." *Christianity Today*, April 10, 1964.

Loomer, Bernard M. "Christian Faith and Process Philosophy." *Process Philosophy and Christian Thought*. Edited by Delwin Brown, *et al*. New York: The Bobbs-Merrill, 1971.

MacGregor, G. H. C. "Principalties and Powers: The Cosmic Background of Paul's Thought." *New Testament Studies*, I, 17−38.

Mackintosh, H. R. *Historic Theories of Atonement, with Comments*. London: Hodder and Stoughton, 1920.

−. *The Christian Experience of Forgiveness*. London: Nisbet and Company, 1927.

Maritain, Jacques. *God and the Permission of Evil*. Milwaukee: Bruce Publishing Company, 1966.

Mascall, E. L. *Existence and Analogy: A Sequel to "He Who Is."* London: Longmans, Green and Company, 1949.

Matthews, W. R. *God: In Christian Thought and Experience*. London: Nisbet and Company, 1930.

McConnell, Francis J. *Is God Limited?* London: Williams and Norgate, 1924.

McIntyre, John. "Analogy." *The Scottish Journal of Theology*, XII (March, 1959), 1−20.

−. *On the Love of God*. London: Collins, 1962.

Michalson, Carl. *Japanese Contributions to Christian Theology*. Philadelphia: The Westminster Press, 1960.

Moltmann, Jürgen. *Theology of Hope*. London: S. C. M. Press, 1967.

Mooney, Christopher F. "Teilhard de Chardin on Suffering and Death." *Journal of Religion and Health* (1965), pp. 429−440.

Mozley, J. K. *The Impassibility of God: A Survey of Christian Thought*. Cambridge: The University Press, 1926.

Muilenburg, James. "The Book of Isaiah (Chapters 40−66)." *The Interpreter's Bible*, V. Edited by George Arthur Buttrick. New York: The Abingdon Press, 1956.

Murphy, John L. *The General Councils of the Church.* Milwaukee: Bruce Publishing Company, 1960.

Murphy, Lois Barclay. *Social Behavior and Child Personality: An Exploratory Study of Some Roots of Sympathy.* New York: Columbia University Press, 1937.

Nelson, J. Robert. "Tolerance, Bigotry and the Christian Faith." *Religion in Life* (Autumn, 1964), pp. 540–558.

–. *The Realm of Redemption: Studies in the Doctrine of the Nature of the Church in Contemporary Protestant Theology.* London: The Epworth Press, 1951.

North, Christopher R. *The Suffering Servant in Deutero-Isaish: An Historical and Critical Study.* London: Oxford University Press, 1956.

Nygren, Anders. *Agape and Eros.* Trans. by Philip S. Watson. Philadelphia: The Westminster Press, 1953.

Oates, Wayne E. *The Revelation of God in Human Suffering.* Philadelphia: The Westminster Press, 1959.

Ockenga, Harold J. *The Spirit of the Living God.* London: Fleming H. Revell Company, 1947.

Origen. *"Homilies in Ezechielem."* *The Early Christian Fathers: A Selection from the Writings of the Fathers from St. Clement of Rome to St. Athanasius.* Edited by Henry Bettenson. London: Oxford University Press, 1956.

Pannenberg, Wolfhart. *Jesus – God and Man.* Trans. by L. L. Wilkins and D. A. Priebe. Philadelphia: The Westminster Press, 1968.

–. *Theology and the Kingdom of God.* Philadelphia: The Westminster Press, 1969.

Pehlmann, Horst Georg. *Analogic entis oder Analogia fidei?: Die Frage der Analogie bei Karl Barth.* Goettingen: Vandenhoeck und Ruprecht, 1965.

Petit, Francis. *The Problem of Evil.* Trans. from the French by Christopher Williams. New York: Hawtorn Books, 1959.

Plato. *The Republic of Plato.* Trans. by Francis M. Cornford. Oxford: The Clarendon Press, 1941.

Pollard, T. E. "The Impassibility of God." *The Scottish Journal of Theology,* VIII (1955), 353–364.

Prenter, Regin. *Spiritus Creator.* Philadelphia: The Muhlenberg Press, 1953.

Proudfoot, C. Merrill. "Imitation or Realistic Participation?: A Study of Paul's Concept of 'Suffering with Christ.'" *Interpretation,* XVII (April, 1963), 140–160.

–. *Suffering: A Christian Understanding.* Philadelphia: The Westminster Press, 1964.

Randles, Marshall. *The Blessed God, Impassibility.* London: Charles H. Kelly, 1900.

Read, Herbert. *The Forms of Things Unknown: Essays Toward an Aesthetic Philosophy.* New York: Horizon Press, 1960.

Reeman, Edmund. *Do We Need a New Idea of God?* Philadelphia: George W. Jacobs and Company, 1917.

Relton, H. Maurice. *A Study in Christology: The Problem of the Relation of the Two Natures in the Person of Christ.* New York: The Macmillan Company, 1931.

–. *Studies in Christian Doctrine.* London: The Macmillan Company, 1960.

Richardson, Alan. *An Introduction to the Theology of the New Testament.* New York: Harper and Brothers, 1958.

–, ed. *Four Anchors From the Stern: Nottingham Reactions to Recent Cambridge Essays.* London: S. C. M. Press, 1963.

Richardson, Cyril C. *The Doctrine of the Trinity.* New York: The Abingdon Press, 1958.

Robinson, H. Wheeler. *The Christian Experience of the Holy Spirit.* New York: Harper and Brothers, 1928.

– . *Suffering, Human and Divine.* New York: The Macmillan Company, 1939.

– . *The Cross in the Old Testament.* London: S. C. M. Press, 1955.

Rose, Margaret E., ed. *The Problem of Suffering: A Collection of Essays Based on a Series of Broadcast Talks for Sixth Forms, Provided by the B. B. C. Under the General Title "The Christian Religion and Its Philosophy".* The British Broadcasting Corporation, 1962.

Scheler, Max. *The Nature of Sympathy.* Trans. by Peter Heath. New Haven: Yale University Press, 1954.

Schweitzer, Albert. *Out of My Life and Thought: An Autobiography.* Trans. by C. T. Campion. New York: H. Holt and Company, 1933.

Scott, Ebenezer. "The True Meaning of Sympathy." *Prize Sermon.* Edited by Edwin A. McAlpin. New York: The Macmillan Company, 1932.

Scroggs, James Rudolf. "Empathy: Aesthetic and Interpersonal." (Ph. D. Dissertation, Boston University, 1963). Ann Arbor: University Microfilms, 1963.

Seeberg, Reinhold. *The Textbook of the History of Christian Doctrines.* 2 vols. Trans. by Charles E. Hay. Grand Rapids: Baker Book House, 1964.

Smart, James. *History and Theology in Second-Isaish: A Commentary on Isaiah 35, 40–66.* Philadelphia: The Westminster Press, 1965.

Smith, T. V., ed. *Philsophers Speak for Themselves: From Aristotle to Plotinus.* Chicago: University of Chicago Press, 1956.

Söderblom, Nathan. *The Mystery of the Cross.* Milwaukee: Morehouse Publishing, 1933).

Soper, David Wesley. *God is Inescapable.* Philadelphia: The Westminster Press, 1959.

Stevenson, J., ed. *A New Eusebius: Documents Illustrative of the History of the Church to A.D. 337.* London: S. P. C. K., 1957.

Streeter, B. H., ed. *God and the Struggle for Existence.* New York: Association Press, 1919.

Streeter, B. H.; and Appasamy, A. J. *The Message of Sadhu Sundar Singh: A Study in Mysticism on Practical Religion.* New York: The Macmillan Company, 1922.

Tasker, R. V. G. *The Biblical Doctrine of the Wrath of God.* London: The Tyndale Press, 1951.

Tertullian. "Against Marcion." *Ante-Nicene Fathers,* III. Edited by Alexander Roberts and James Donaldson. Grand Rapids: Wm. B. Eerdmans Publishing Company, 1957.

– . "Against Praxeas." *Ante-Nicene Fathers,* III. Edited by Alexander Roberts and James Donaldson. Grand Rapids: Wm. B. Eerdmans Publishing Company, 1957.

Thomas Aquinas. *Summa Theologica: Latin Text and English Translation, Introductions, Notes, Appendices and Glossaries,* I. New York: McGraw-Hill Book Company, Inc., 1964.

Thomas, George. *Christian Ethics and Moral Philosophy.* New York: Charles Scribner's Sons, 1955.

Tillich, Paul. *Systematic Theology.* 3 vols. Chicago: University of Chicago Press, 1951–1963.

– . *Love, Power, and Justice.* New York: Oxford University Press, 1954.

Von Balthasar, Hans Urs. *Karl Barth: Darstellung und Deutung seiner Theologie.* Koeln: Verlag Jakob Hegner, 1950.

Von Hügel, Baron Friedrich. "Morals and Religion." *Essays and Addresses on the Philosophy of Religion,* Second Series. London: J. M. Dent and Sons, 1926.

Wenley, R. M. *Stoicism and Its Influence.* New York: Longmans, Green and Company, 1927.

Weatherhead, Leslie D. *Why Do Men Suffer?* New York: The Abingdon Press, 1936.

Whitehead, Alfred North. *Symbolism, Its Meaning and Effect.* New York: The Macmillan Company, 1927.

–. *Process and Reality.* New York: The Macmillan Company, 1929.

Wolf, William J. *No Cross, No Crown: A Study of the Atonement.* New York: Doubleday, 1957.

Woodson, Joseph Franklin. "The Meaning and Development of Empathy." (Ph. D. Dissertation, Boston University, 1954). Ann Arbor: University Microfilms, 1954.

Woolcombe, Kenneth J. "The Pain of God." *The Scottish Journal of Theology,* XX, No. 2 (June, 1967), 129–148.

INDEX

112

DATE DUE